AN ANTIDOTE FOR INJUSTICE

AN ANTIDOTE FOR INJUSTICE

A NEW PARADIGM FOR WINNING "OLD" SEXUAL ABUSE CASES AGAINST COMPLICIT PRIVATE SCHOOLS

KEVIN THOMAS MULHEARN

HARD NOCK PRESS

NEW YORK

An Antidote for Injustice: A New Paradigm for Winning "Old" Sexual Abuse Cases Against Complicit Private Schools

Published in the United States of America by
Hard Nock Press, LLC

Hard Nock Press, LLC
P.O. Box 665
Orangeburg, NY 10962
www.hardnockpress.com

Printed in the United States of America

10 9 8 7 6 5 4 3 2 1

ISBN: 978-0-615-85139-6

First Edition

DEDICATION

For my mother, Mary Ann Mulhearn, whose beautiful and compassionate heart is always filled with child-like wonder and enthusiasm. Thank you, Mom, for your unwavering love, belief, and support.

- and -

In loving memory of my father, Thomas Lee Mulhearn, whose inimitable fighting spirit continues to inspire me to always give my best. This son wanted nothing more than to make his Dad proud.

* * *

This book is also dedicated to twelve sexual abuse survivors from my alma mater, Poly Prep, who, having endured unimaginable horrors, still somehow found the courage to battle for truth, peace, justice, and happiness. Thank you, my friends, for fighting the good fight, for teaching me many lessons, and for helping to lead us all to our better angels.

DISCLAIMER

This book is designed to provide information on various legal issues raised in school sex abuse cover-up cases. It is sold with the understanding that the publisher and author are not engaged in rendering legal or other professional services. If you require legal assistance, you should seek the services of a competent attorney.

Every effort has been made to make this book as complete and accurate as possible. However, there may be mistakes, both typographical and in content. This text, therefore, should be used only as a general guide and not as the ultimate source of information. Furthermore, this book contains information (and a description of law) that is current only up to the printing date.

The author and publisher shall have neither liability nor responsibility to any person or entity with respect to any loss or damage caused, or alleged to have been caused, directly or indirectly, by the information contained in this book.

ACKNOWLEDGMENTS

I was introduced to the legal issues pertaining to sexual abuse in schools by the intrepid warriors, John Joseph Paggioli, David Hiltbrand, James Zimmerman and Philip Culhane. I deeply thank these special men—each a tower of strength in the fight for justice—for their support, encouragement and friendship.

I also thank my tenacious research assistant, Thomas Butterworth, for his hard work and positive attitude, my outstanding and always cheerful legal assistant, Sally Riley, for her patience in typing dozens of drafts, my friend and business manager, Brian Lane, for his acumen in keeping me in the good graces of my creditors, my friend and colleague, Michael Kalmus, Esq., for reviewing this book and contributing an excellent foreword, and my friend, Mordechai Twersky, for his incisive and expeditious editorial suggestions.

Last but not least, I extend heartfelt thanks and appreciation to my wife, Roxanne, for taking exemplary care of our child those many evenings and weekends during which I was busy conducting research or putting pen to paper.

TABLE OF CONTENTS

CHAPTER II

**Viable Actions Based Upon Pre-Abuse
Misrepresentations**

___

FOREWORD

Law is the constant and perpetual will to allot every man his due.

— Domitus Ulpian

Victims of sexual abuse are among the most reticent of litigants. They are children who typically spend years trying to repress horrible memories while suffering in silence. They often share their most intimate demons with no one, be it the result of being raised in a broken home (as many victims are), the fear of confiding in authority figures (who, in many instances turn out to be the abusers), or the shame associated with the mistaken belief that the victim is somehow to blame for someone else's crime. Reaching the age of majority, which typically triggers the running of the statute of limitations for the filing of a suit, does nothing to quell those internal demons, and many otherwise viable lawsuits are never filed.

Regardless of the justification for delay, the statute of limitations for a potential plaintiff to file suit against his or her abuser generally commences when the victim reaches the age of majority (18) and expires several years later. The rationale is simple and direct: the identity of the defendant is known and the acts forming the basis of the suit are known at the time they are committed; thus, any suit brought in response must be brought within the limitations period in order to be viable.

What rules apply, however, when the identity of an additional potential defendant is NOT readily known, as the result of silence, subterfuge or conspiracy? What rights does a victim possess when he discovers, often years after the expiration of the applicable statute of limitations, that his school, church, synagogue, or other institution KNEW about predatory conduct on the part of an employee or administrator prior to the date of his own abuse, but did nothing to stop it? How are the rights of victims impacted when these same institutions act to hide the evidence of their prior knowledge of, and indifference to, the predators in their midst?

These are among the most fiercely contested questions in New York jurisprudence today, pitting powerful and highly influential interests who strenuously argue that cases of abuse, sometimes decades old, can never be viable against a school or religious institution, regardless of the action (or inaction) involved, against thousands of victims, most unknown, who discover, long after their initial victimization, that both the identity and proclivity of their abuser was known to a trusted entity that failed, for whatever reason, to protect the children under its care and then acted to hide the evidence of its own knowledge and failure to act in the hope that the passage of time would render it immune from consequence.

In *An Antidote For Injustice*, Kevin Mulhearn provides a playbook for the victims and lays out a powerful case for holding truly culpable institutions responsible *under existing law*, an argument seen as extremely daunting or even impossible to make by many within the legal community.

Kevin Mulhearn is part of a dying breed of lawyers, a single practitioner/litigator willing to take on the riskiest of cases with the passion of a zealot and the ferocious willingness to successfully challenge long held assumptions. Although well-positioned for a comfortable and lucrative career in "big law," Mulhearn instead opted for the road less traveled. He resisted the lure of high-powered New York City law firms and chose to open a one man shop in the suburbs of Rockland County. In part as a result of Mulhearn's low-profile address, his adversaries have consistently underestimated both his ability and capacity to take on—and often win—the toughest of cases against the most formidable opposition. With a bar-room brawler style that often belies his effusive Irish charm, Mulhearn sometimes seems like a character created from the mind of a Damon Runyon or Dashiell Hammett. In reality, all characterizations aside, he's just a damn good lawyer. I say that from the unique perspective of someone who has been both an adversary and a colleague.

With an eye for nuance and the rhetorical force and consistency of a true believer willing and able to exhaust his ammunition to make his case, Kevin Mulhearn stands the so-called "conventional wisdom" on institutional responsibility for the sexual abuse of children on its head. *An Antidote For Injustice* should be required reading for anyone with an interest or stake in this hot button issue.

— Michael Kalmus, Esq.

PREFACE

The strictest law sometimes becomes the severest injustice.

— Benjamin Franklin

In 2005, John Joseph Paggioli ("Paggioli"), then forty-seven years old, filed a lawsuit in the Kings County Supreme Court against Poly Prep Country Day School ("Poly Prep"), a well-regarded private school in Brooklyn, New York.[1] Paggioli claimed that from 1970 to 1974 he was repeatedly sexually abused by Poly Prep's revered—and by then deceased—football coach, Philip Foglietta. Paggioli alleged that numerous administrators and faculty members conspired to cover up the school's knowledge of Foglietta's propensity to sexually assault boys. Paggioli filed a claim for, *inter alia*, negligent retention and supervision.

On January 5, 2006, the Honorable Lewis L. Douglass (since retired) issued a three page Decision and Order which dismissed Paggioli's case in its entirety.[2] Justice Douglass, in what could fairly be described as a less than sophisticated analysis of the implicated issues, stated: "In my view, this case is simply too old."[3]

---

[1] *Paggioli v. Poly Prep, CDS*, Index No. 11188/05 (Sup. Ct. Kings Cty.).
[2] *See Zimmerman v. Poly Prep, CDS*, Case 1:09-CV-04586-FB-CLP (EDNY) (Document 198-1).
[3] *Id.* at 4.

Paggioli, after learning of additional facts which supported his supposition that the school had engaged in a cover-up of Foglietta's sexual misconduct, amended his Complaint. After extensive briefing, on October 25, 2006, Justice Douglass issued a one page Order—written by hand in a barely legible cursive—which provided that his January 5, 2006 Decision and Order "covers the Amended Complaint as well."[4] Again, Paggioli's case was summarily dismissed because it was "too old."[5]

The *Paggioli* case is far from unique. Recent history has revealed that a multitude of schools, including many with sterling reputations, have engaged in a long-term cover-up of sexual abuse committed by faculty members against students. When the cover-ups are at long last exposed, these schools then usually sprint behind the prophylactic shield of the statutes of limitation. The schools and their defenders argue that these cases, horrific as they may be, are time-barred.

---

[4] *See Zimmerman v. Poly Prep, CDS*, Case 1:09-CV-04586-FB-CLP (EDNY) (Document 198-2 at 2).

[5] *See id.* Paggioli, incensed that the Court did not bother to even use type-script for such a momentous (at least for him) Order, henceforth referred to the Court's October 25, 2006 Order as "the crayon decision." Paggioli later became one of the original seven plaintiffs who filed suit against Poly Prep in the Eastern District of New York in October 2009. (*Zimmerman v. Poly Prep, CDS*, Case No.: 1:09-CV-04586-FB-CLP). Five more plaintiffs were added to this case before it was resolved in December 2012.

This strategy has usually been successful, as hundreds of sex abuse victims have been denied legal redress because they waited too long to file suit. Many judges who issue these dismissal orders fail to consider, or minimize, the distinct possibility that many of these late-filed cases are so "old" because, for several decades, the schools have been successful in their conspiracies and cover-ups of their employees' rapes and sexual assaults of numerous children.

This book, which focuses on New York law,[6] seeks to demonstrate that many of these "old" school sexual abuse cases may well still be viable. To breathe life into these "old dogs," the inaccurate label too often pinned on these cases, it is necessary to teach the naysayers some new tricks. Yet, the legal theories proposed in this book do not appear magically from whole cloth. Quite the contrary, each theory is based on well-settled legal rules and one overriding principle: the law should be a vehicle for justice, rather than a mechanism for schools to betray the children in their charge—in the most vile of ways—and still escape unscathed.

---

[6] Chapter IV, which discusses sex abuse cover-up claims brought against schools under Title IX, has broader applicability.

INTRODUCTION

As numerous headlines over the last few years have made clear, a tragic pattern too often repeats itself: a revered teacher or coach at an esteemed private school sexually abuses or rapes numerous innocent students. These victims suffer their abuse in silence. Paralyzed by a toxic brew of fear, shame, and embarrassment, they tuck away their pain and tell no one. Then, after decades of dealing with numerous abuse-related psychological problems, such as severe depression, fear of intimacy, failure to trust, and/or drug and alcohol addictions or dependencies, they finally find the emotional strength to speak out about their abuse and abuser. When they do, abuse allegations from other former students begin to surface. The victims then discover, to their surprise and horror, that numerous sexual abuse complaints against the offending teacher or coach had been made to high-ranking school administrators both prior to and after their own abuse.

These school administrators, though, made the fateful decision to protect the brand of the school and the reputation of the abuser over the physical and emotional well-being of the children entrusted to the school's care. The school administrators did not notify former or current students, or their parents, that credible abuse claims against the teacher or coach had been made. Nor did they contact law enforcement authorities. Instead, they allowed their child rapist employee to continue to pick off his unsuspecting prey at will, garner the respect and admiration of the school community, and ultimately retire (or transfer to another school) amidst the din of saccharine praise and under the weight of undeserved honors.

The prevailing wisdom provides that in New York State victims of sexual abuse who discover a school's cover-up for a known sexual predator decades after their own abuse are without legal recourse. The Statute of Limitations, according to this view, is sacrosanct. This mindset, which is based upon a fundamental misunderstanding of discovery rules governing accrual of claims and the equitable estoppel doctrine, and the misapplication and under-utilization of fraud elements and principles, is wrong. Unfortunately, in sex abuse cases, a series of wrong-headed and legally tenuous presumptions (on admittedly complex issues) have tilted courts towards early dismissal of older sex abuse claims. These erroneous premises, borne of confusion and the distortion of prior case law, have infected practically every state or federal court in New York State which has analyzed the timeliness issues in the many "old" sexual abuse claims which have proliferated over the last few decades.

The goals of this book are to shed the existing cloak of misapprehension and confusion for potential litigants, attorneys, and judges; provide the correct analytical foundation for the governing principles; and demonstrate that schools and school administrators which knowingly condone, facilitate, and/or cover up the sexual abuse of children by school employees cannot properly escape liability by scurrying behind the statute of limitations shield.

Chapter I of this book demonstrates that plaintiffs should be able to invoke equitable estoppel, which stops the statutes of limitation from running, if they can plausibly allege that school officials made affirmative misrepresentations or otherwise engaged in overt acts of fraud or deception *after* plaintiffs were abused (and within plaintiffs' limitation periods). Moreover, the unique *in loco parentis* supervisory standard that New York law imposes on schools should permit courts to be more willing to recognize tolling misrepresentations made by school officials to children about school safety and faculty credentials, character, and trustworthiness.

In a similar vein, Chapter II demonstrates that survivors of sexual abuse who discover school cover-ups or conspiracies years or even decades after their own sexual abuse may be able to assert viable causes of action for fraudulent misrepresentation and negligent misrepresentation under New York common law. These misrepresentation claims (which must be based on school conduct that occurred *before* plaintiffs were sexually abused) may invoke the fraud statute of limitations [New York CPLR ("CPLR") § 213(8)], which delays accrual—the running of the statute of limitations–until the time a plaintiff knows or could have known through reasonable diligence of the fraud sued upon.[7]

Chapter III shows that sexual abuse survivors may invoke several New York consumer protection laws (New York General Business Law §§ 349 & 350) and assert viable claims based on the alleged "deceptive acts or practices" and/or "false advertising" of culpable schools. These claims are based on the premise that a school engaged in actionable deception if it represented to students and their parents that a school was safe, and the faculty trustworthy, when school officials knew that a dangerous sexual predator employee would be given easy access to unsuspecting children.

---

[7] Under CPLR § 213(8), a plaintiff must file suit no later than six years after the fraud occurred or two years from when she discovered or could have discovered the fraud.

Finally, Chapter IV provides a detailed account as to how Title IX and the federal discovery rule which delays accrual of federal claims that borrow state statutes of limitations (including Title IX), may permit otherwise time-barred plaintiffs to obtain legal redress against schools (and only schools) that engage in sex abuse cover-ups. These federal claims may open the federal courthouse doors to aggrieved sex abuse survivors.

I.   VIABLE NEGLIGENT RETENTION AND SUPERVISION ACTIONS BASED UPON POST-ABUSE MISCONDUCT WHERE EQUITABLE ESTOPPEL MAY BE INVOKED

A.   Basic Statute of Limitations Principles

"At common law there was no fixed time for the bringing of an action. Personal actions were merely confined to the joint lifetimes of the parties."[8] In the wake of the Civil War, however, after numerous state legislatures had enacted laws setting time limits for various actions, the United States Supreme Court noted that statutes of limitation "are founded upon the general experience of mankind that claims, which are valid, are not usually allowed to be neglected. The lapse of years without any attempt to enforce a demand creates, therefore, a presumption against its original validity, or that it has ceased to subsist. This presumption is made by these statutes a positive bar; and they thus become statutes of repose, protecting parties from the prosecution of stale claims, when, by loss of evidence from death of some witnesses, and the imperfect recollection of others, or the destruction of documents, it might be impossible to establish the truth."[9]

Statutes of limitations are thus a legislative creation designed "to afford protection to defendants against defending stale claims after a reasonable period of time had elapsed during which a person of ordinary diligence would bring an action."[10]

---

[8] *Flanagan v. Mount Eden General Hosp.*, 24 N.Y.2d 427, 429 (1969).

[9] *Riddlesbarger v. Hartford Ins. Co.*, 74 U.S. 386, 390 (1868).

[10] *Flanagan*, 24 N.Y.2d at 429; *see also, Tuper v. Tuper,* 98 A.D.3d 55, 58 (4th Dept. 2012).

While statutes of limitation derive from a public policy to make persons secure in their reasonable expectations "that the slate has been wiped clean of ancient obligations,"[11] they are designed to foster, not hinder, litigants' search for "the truth."[12] That fundamental tenet, which has been ignored by many courts which have addressed so-called "old" sex abuse cases, underscores most of the legal issues discussed in this book.

Statutes of limitation must be distinguished from pure statutes of repose. Statutes of repose, commonly used for comprehensive products liability codifications, begin to run when a specific event takes place, regardless of whether a potential claim has accrued or even whether any injury has occurred.[13] "The repose period serves as an absolute barrier that prevents a plaintiff's right of action. In other words, the period of repose has the effect of preventing what might otherwise have been a cause of action from ever arising."[14]   Statutes of repose "envelop both the right and the remedy" and practically block[ ] causes of action before they even accrue."[15]

In contrast, a statute of limitations "cannot begin to run until the plaintiff's claim has accrued."[16] In New York, therefore, the expiration of the time period prescribed in a Statute of Limitations "does not wipe out the substantive right; it merely suspends the remedy."[17] As such, in New York statutes of

---

[11] *Flanagan*, 24 N.Y.2d at 429 (*citing, Developments in the Law: Statutes of Limitation*, 63 Harv. L. Rev. 1177, 1185 (1950)).

[12] *Riddlesbarger*, 74 U.S. at 390.

[13] *Tanges v. Heidelberg North America, Inc.*, 93 N.Y.2d 48, 55 (1999).

[14] *Id. (quoting, 4 American Law of Products Liability* 3d § 47:55, at 88 (emphasis in original)).

[15] *Id.* (citations omitted).

[16] *City of Pontiac General Employees' Retirement System v. MBIA, Inc.*, 637 F.3d 169, 176 (2d. Cir. 2011).

[17] *Tanges*, 93 N.Y. 2d at 55 (*quoting*, Siegel, *N.Y. Practice* § 34, at 38

limitation "are generally considered procedural[.]"[18]

The old stand-by for plaintiffs asserting claims against schools for facilitating their sexual abuse by a school employee is a negligent retention and supervision claim.[19] In New York, negligent supervision and retention claims are subject to the general three year statute of limitations for personal injury actions.[20] The general rule in New York for negligence actions "is that the Statute of Limitations starts to run when the cause of action accrues,"[21] and that "a cause of action accrues from the date of the injury."[22]

If a person is abused as a minor, he or she receives the benefit of the toll for infancy created by CPLR § 208, which permits a person to bring a claim within "three years after the disability [of infancy] ceases." This means that a person sexually abused as a child must bring a negligent retention and supervision claim against his or her school before he or she turns twenty-one; otherwise, a belated claim—filed by anyone twenty-one years of age or older—will be *prima facie* untimely.

(2d. ed.)).

[18] *Id.*

[19] "To state a claim for negligent supervision or retention under New York law, in addition to the standard elements of negligence, i.e., duty, breach, causation, and injury, a plaintiff must show: (1) that the tort-feasor and the defendants were in an employee-employer relationship; (2) that the employer knew or should have known of the employee's propensity for the conduct which caused the injury prior to the injury's occurrence; and (3) that the tort was committed on the employer's premises or with the employer's chattels." *Dunahoo v. Hewlett-Packard Co.*, 2012 WL 178332, *3 (SDNY 2012) (*quoting, Ehrens v. Lutheran Church*, 385 F.3d 232, 235 (2d Cir. 2004)).

[20] CPLR § 214(5).

[21] *Woodlaurel, Inc. v. Wittman*, 199 A.D.2d 497, 498 (2d Dept. 1993).

[22] *Brooklyn Union Gas Co. v. Hunter Turbo Corp.*, 241 A.D.2d 505, 506 (2d Dept. 1997).

B.   Basic Equitable Estoppel Principles

"A defendant who seeks dismissal of a complaint pursuant to CPLR [§] 3211 (a)(5) on the ground that it is barred by the statute of limitations bears the initial burden of proving, *prima facie*, that the time in which to commence an action has expired."[23] If a defendant meets that threshold, "[t]he burden then shifts to the plaintiff to aver evidentiary facts establishing that his or her cause of action falls within an exception to the statute of limitation, or raising an issue of fact as to whether such an exception applies."[24]

If a claim is *prima facie* untimely, a plaintiff may thus still overcome the statute of limitations if he pleads sufficient facts for equitable estoppel, otherwise known as equitable tolling, to apply. New York courts have the power, both at law and equity, to bar the assertion of the affirmative defense of the statute of limitations where it is "the defendant's affirmative wrongdoing which produced the long delay between the accrual of the cause of action and the institution of the legal proceeding."[25]   New York law thus recognizes the doctrine of equitable tolling (otherwise known as equitable estoppel), which can overcome a statute of limitations defense "where a plaintiff was induced by fraud, misrepresentations or deception to refrain from filing a timely action."[26]

Under New York law, however, "equitable estoppel does not apply where the misrepresentation or act of concealment underlying the estoppel claim is the same act which forms the

---

[23] *Texeria v. BAB Nuclear Radiology, P.C.*, 43 A.D.3d 403, 405 (2d Dept. 2007); *see also, Gravel v. Cicola*, 297 A.D.2d 620, 620-21 (2d Dept. 2002).

[24] *Id.; see also, Gravel*, 297 A.D.2d at 621.

[25] *See General Stencils v. Chiappa*, 18 N.Y.2d 125, 128 (1966).

[26] *Simcuski v. Saeli*, 44 N.Y.2d 442, 449 (1978).

basis of plaintiff's underlying cause of action."[27] Instead, for equitable estoppel to be invoked, a plaintiff must establish that a defendant made fraudulent misrepresentations or otherwise engaged in overt misconduct—*after his initial wrongdoing*—which prevented plaintiff from commencing her action on time.[28] "The doctrine of equitable estoppel ... [thus] comes into play when some conduct by a defendant *after his initial wrongdoing* has prevented plaintiff from discovering or suing upon the initial wrong."[29]

The equitable estoppel doctrine, pursuant to New York common law, thus provides that if a plaintiff alleges fraudulent concealment which occurred prior to or concurrent with the cause of action sued upon, he may not invoke equitable estoppel or equitable tolling to stop or toll the applicable statute of limitations.

If, however, a plaintiff's complaint sounds in fraud, then he can invoke the fraud diligence-discovery rule, CPLR § 213(8), which provides that a plaintiff must sue for fraud no later than two (2) years from the date he discovered, or with reasonable diligence could have discovered, the fraud. A plaintiff's fraud claim in New York thus accrues (i.e., the statute of limitations starts to run) only when he discovers or could (through reasonable diligence) have discovered the fraud.[30]

---

[27] *See Abercrombie v. Andrew College*, 438 F. Supp.2d 243, 265 (SDNY 2006) (*quoting, Kaufman v. Cohen*, 307 A.D.2d 113, 122 (1st Dept. 2003)); *see also, Ross v. Louise Wise Services, Inc.*, 8 N.Y.3d 478, 491 (2d Dept. 2007).

[28] *Abercrombie*, 438 F. Supp.2d at 265; *Ross*, 8 N.Y.3d at 491 (*citing, Zumpano v. Quinn*, 6 N.Y.3d 666 (2006); *Rizk v. Cohen*, 73 N.Y.2d 98, 105-06 (1989)).

[29] *Smith v. Smith*, 830 F.2d 11, 13 (2d Cir. 1987)(emphasis added).

[30] *See* Chapter II.F, *infra*.

C.   The *Zumpano* Decision: Equitable Estoppel Cannot Be Invoked Without Post-Abuse Allegations of Fraud, Misrepresentations, or Deception

In 2006 the New York Court of Appeals, in *Zumpano v. Quinn*,[31] considered appeals in two consolidated actions: *Zumpano*[32] and *Boyle v. Smith*. In *Boyle*, forty-two plaintiffs contended that the Diocese of Brooklyn and several bishops should be equitably estopped from asserting the statute of limitations because the bishops and the Diocese were aware that certain priests had sexually abused children and yet engaged in a corrupt campaign and pattern of concealment.[33] The *Boyle* plaintiffs pled that defendants failed to investigate and report the conduct to law enforcement authorities, transferred abusive priests to different parishes, and made secret payments to victims and their families in return for their silence.[34]

Yet the *Zumpano* Court refused to equitably toll plaintiffs' negligence claims because plaintiffs failed to establish "that subsequent and specific actions by defendants somehow kept them from timely bringing suit."[35] Focusing on plaintiffs' allegations that the *Boyle* church defendants had actively concealed their knowledge of various priests' sexual abuse of children, the *Zumpano* Court emphasized that concealment, without post-abuse affirmative wrongdoing by defendants, was

---

[31] 6 N.Y.3d 666 (2006).

[32] The *Zumpano* plaintiff sought to equitably toll the Statute of Limitations pursuant to the CPLR § 208 toll for insanity. The Court of Appeals rejected this basis for tolling because plaintiff failed to prove that he suffered from an ongoing disability which rendered him incapable of protecting his legal rights. *Id.* at 677.

[33] *Id.* at 672.

[34] *Id.*

[35] *Id.* at 674.

insufficient to trigger equitable estoppel:

> It is not enough that plaintiffs alleged defendants were aware of the abuse and remained silent about it ... A wrongdoer is not legally obliged to make a public confession, or to alert people who may have claims against it, to get the benefit of a statute of limitations. *Plaintiffs do not allege any specific misrepresentation to them by defendants*, or any deceptive conduct sufficient to constitute a basis for equitable estoppel. Nor is there any indication that further discovery would yield such information. *No new separate and subsequent acts of wrongdoing beyond the sexually abusive acts themselves are alleged*, and equitable estoppel is therefore inapplicable to these cases.[36]

As a separate basis for equitable estoppel, the *Boyle* plaintiffs argued that defendants breached a fiduciary duty owed to them by concealing their own actions in covering up the abuse.[37] Plaintiffs relied on the rule set forth by the Second Department in *Gleason v. Spota*, that "[w]here concealment without actual misrepresentation is claimed to have prevented plaintiff from commencing a timely action, the plaintiff must demonstrate a fiduciary relationship ... which gave the defendant an obligation to inform him or her of facts underlying the claim."[38]

The *Zumpano* Court dismantled plaintiffs' concealment argument. The Court emphasized that plaintiffs knew they had been abused, knew the identity of their abusers, and knew that

---

[36] *Id.* at 674-75 (emphasis added).

[37] *Id.* at 675.

[38] *Gleason v. Spota*, 194 A.D.2d 764, 765 (2d Dept. 1993).

the abusers were employed by the diocese.[39] Accordingly, plaintiffs failed to demonstrate that defendants' failure to inform them of certain facts contributed to their delay in filing suit.[40] Moreover, "[p]laintiffs possessed timely knowledge of the actual misconduct and the relationship between the priests and their respective dioceses *to make inquiry and ascertain relevant facts* prior to the running of the statute of limitations."[41]

Zumpano thus imputed the dioceses' knowledge of prior bad acts by the offending priests to the plaintiffs under the rationale that plaintiffs—had they conducted an inquiry at any time from their abuse until they turned twenty-one— would have ascertained enough facts to file viable negligent retention and supervision claims against the dioceses.[42] Plaintiffs, according to this logic, would have learned from the diocese that it had actual or constructive knowledge that certain priests had a propensity to sexually abuse children yet failed to notify the police and continued to place these priests in positions of trust with scores of children. The *Zumpano* Court saw no irony in its tacit but critical finding that the church defendants, credibly accused of a decades-long conspiracy to conceal information related to the sexual abuse of children by pederast priests who were often reassigned to different parishes after abuse allegations surfaced, would have been open and candid had plaintiffs made specific inquiries about their abusers.[43]

---

[39] *Zumpano*, 6 N.Y.3d at 676.

[40] *Id.*

[41] *Id.* (emphasis added).

[42] *See id.*

[43] The *Boyle* plaintiffs (in their amended complaint (at para. 115)) quoted Bishop Wilton D. Gregory, former President of the United States Conference of Catholic Bishops, who stated: "We are the ones, whether through ignorance or lack of vigilance, or—God forbid—with knowledge, who allowed priest abusers to remain in ministry and reassigned them to

Zumpano's imputation of knowledge to plaintiffs is premised on its key finding that plaintiffs did not sufficiently allege that the church defendants had made any affirmative misrepresentations to plaintiffs about their abusers or defendants' knowledge of complaints against their abusers, or otherwise engaged in fraud or deception, within the applicable limitations periods.[44]

The conduct which plaintiffs claimed gave rise to the estoppel was thus exclusively the alleged fiduciary relationship between the offending priests and the child victims. Accordingly, assuming that such a fiduciary relationship—which triggered an obligation by defendants to disclose relevant facts within their knowledge—existed, plaintiffs were required "to proceed with their lawsuit, or at least with an inquiry into the facts, within the statutory limitations period computed from the time 'the conduct relied on [as a basis for equitable estoppel] cease[d] to be operational.'"[45] The alleged breach of fiduciary duty, therefore, could not "estop defendants from relying on the time that elapsed after the alleged fiduciary relationship no longer existed."[46]

Zumpano sounds a virtual death knell for all equitable estoppel claims in *prima facie* untimely sex abuse cases which sound in negligence where the alleged misconduct is exclusively concealment and the alleged duty to disclose stems from a

---

communities where they continued to abuse. We are the ones who chose not to report the criminal actions of priests to the authorities, because the law did not require this. We are the ones who worried more about the possibility of scandal than in bringing about the kind of openness that helps prevent abuse. And we are the ones who, at times, responded to victims and their families as adversaries and not as suffering members of the Church." *Zumpano*, 6 N.Y.3d at 685 (G.B. Smith, dissenting).

[44] *Id.* at 675. *See* Chapter I.D-G, *infra*.

[45] *Zumpano*, 6 N.Y.3d at 676 (*quoting, Simcuski*, 44 N.Y.2d at 450).

[46] *Id.*

fiduciary *relationship*. Several cases decided after *Zumpano* confirm the futility of this type of equitable estoppel argument.[47] The end of the *relationship* between institution and child signals the end of any estoppel and begins the running of the statute of limitations anew.

In the school context, for a plaintiff to successfully invoke equitable estoppel in order to save a *prima facie* untimely negligent retention and supervision case from being dismissed as time-barred, he must therefore plead and prove that school administrators made affirmative misrepresentations to him (or otherwise engaged in overt acts of fraud and/or deception) *after* he was abused, and that in reliance on those misrepresentations (or overt misconduct) he refrained from filing a lawsuit against the school and its culpable administrators.[48] With but one notable exception,[49] New York courts have been extremely reluctant to recognize affirmative misrepresentations which will trigger equitable estoppel. Such reticence is misplaced.

As this book explains, courts may rely upon several affirmative misrepresentation theories which will justify the equitable tolling of negligent retention and supervision claims against schools which covered up sexual abuse by their employees. These misrepresentations, moreover, if they occurred *prior* to a plaintiff's sexual abuse by a known abuser, and were then concealed by school officials, may also serve as the bases for several independent tort actions against the culpable schools and school officials.

---

[47] *See, e.g., Walker v. Lorch*, 2013 WL 3348013 (SDNY 2013); *Franco v. Roman Catholic Diocese of Las Vegas,* 24 Misc. 3d 1205(A), 889 N.Y.S.2d 882 (Table), 2009 WL 1777146, *2 (Sup. Ct. Queens Cty. 2009); *Doe v. Kolko* 2008 WL 4146199, *5-6 n.3 (EDNY 2008) (citations omitted).

[48] *See Zimmerman v. Poly Prep, CDS*, 888 F. Supp.2d 317, 340 (EDNY 2012).

[49] *Id.*

D.   Negligent Misrepresentations Can Invoke Equitable Estoppel

New York law provides that "a party may not, even innocently, mislead an opponent and then claim the benefit of the deception."[50] As the *Zumpano* Court stated, equitable estoppel will apply "where plaintiff was induced by fraud, misrepresentations or deception to refrain from filing a timely action."[51]

Zumpano does not state or suggest that the "misrepresentations" referenced must be fraudulent misrepresentations. To the contrary, the Court's enumeration of "fraud" and "misrepresentations" as independent trigger points for equitable estoppel suggests that a negligent misrepresentation with risk of physical harm will toll *prima facie* untimely claims until the time a plaintiff discovers the negligent misrepresentation.

E.   The *Zimmerman* "Game-Changer": Affirmative Misrepresentations About a Teacher or Coach in School Publications or at School Events Which Conceal Essential Elements of a Cause of Action May Invoke Equitable Estoppel

In *Zimmerman v. Poly Prep, CDS*,[52] Senior Judge Frederic Block, citing several cases in other jurisdictions, stated that "affirmative misrepresentations or deceitful conduct designed to keep a potential plaintiff from gaining knowledge of an essential element

---

[50] *Romano v. Metropolitan Life Insur. Co.*, 271 N.Y. 288, 293 (1936); *Triple Cities Constr. Co. v. Maryland Casualty Co.*, 4 N.Y.2d 443, 448 (1958); *see also, Bucon, Inc. v. Pennsylvania Manufacturing Assoc. Insur. Co.*, 151 A.D.2d 207, 211 (3d Dept. 1989).

[51] 6 N.Y.3d at 674 (citation omitted).

[52] 888 F. Supp.2d 317 (EDNY 2012).

of a viable cause of action for a claim of negligent retention or supervision by an employer of a sexual predator-employee [is] a game-changer."[53]

Zimmerman, therefore, was "qualitatively distinguish[ed]" from *Zumpano* because the *Zimmerman* plaintiffs alleged that Poly Prep engaged in an affirmative course of conduct during the period of limitation to deceive the plaintiffs into believing that they had no claim against Poly Prep because the school had no knowledge of its sexual predator employee's wrongdoing, even though several students had complained to school administrators about the employee's sexual abuse.[54]

The *Zimmerman* plaintiffs alleged that Poly Prep affirmatively misrepresented, at school events they attended and in school publications they received, that the subject employee "remained in good standing" and "was held in high regard."[55] Thus, Poly Prep, by holding out the employee as a reputable and esteemed teacher throughout the limitations period, engaged in deceitful conduct which might plausibly have led plaintiffs to falsely believe that Poly Prep was unaware of the sexual predator employee's misconduct and could not be liable for negligent retention or supervision.[56]

In *Zimmerman*, Judge Block also held that to successfully invoke equitable estoppel plaintiffs would still have to prove justifiable reliance (i.e., that their justifiable reliance upon the misrepresentations was the reason why they did not timely file actions against the school) and due diligence (i.e., that their actions were brought within a reasonable time after the facts giving rise to the estoppel ceased to be operational).[57]

---

[53] *Id.* at 339 (citations omitted).

[54] *Id.* at 340.

[55] *Id.*

[56] *Id.*

[57] *Id.* at 341. Judge Block ordered an evidentiary hearing to resolve these

Individuals who were abused by a teacher or coach after one or more school administrators received actual knowledge that said teacher or coach had a propensity to sexually abuse children (i.e., after the school received complaints about an employee's conduct), can follow the *Zimmerman* framework and successfully invoke equitable estoppel if the school continued to keep a known sexual abuser on staff.

To succeed, plaintiffs must plausibly allege that the school, during the limitations periods, affirmatively represented to each of the plaintiffs, at school events they attended and in school publications they received, that the teacher or coach at issue remained in good standing, demonstrated strong character, was trustworthy, and was held in high regard by the school and its administrators. Plaintiffs must also plausibly allege that they relied upon these representations in refraining from filing a lawsuit against the school, and that they filed their negligent retention and supervision claims no later than three years after they learned of the school's misrepresentations.[58] If there is some credible evidence that the school had prior knowledge of plaintiffs' abuser's propensity for abuse, the above type of allegations should be sufficient for plaintiffs' negligent retention and supervision claims to invoke equitable estoppel.

---

threshold equitable estoppel issues, *see id.*, but the case was resolved prior to the scheduled hearing.

[58] *See* Chapter I.F, *infra*.

F.   Tolling Based on Misrepresentations: The Statute Starts to Run Only When a Plaintiff Learns of the Misrepresentations

As the Eastern District of New York Court recently held in *Bild v. Weider*, [59] "where an estoppel to assert the statute of limitations is made out [through fraud, misrepresentations and/or deception], then…the question most critical to a statute of limitations defense—when did the limitations period expire—loses its determinative significance[.]"[60]

In that event, the key question for a court then becomes "was the action commenced within a reasonable time *after the facts giving rise to the estoppel ceased to be operational.*"[61] This requires a court to determine first, as a matter of fact, when the deception ceased to be operational, and second, as a matter of law, what constitutes a reasonable period of time in which to have commenced an action[.]"[62]

If a plaintiff can credibly claim that school officials made any affirmative "misrepresentations" to him during his limitations periods, he can thus equitably toll all legal claims arising from those misrepresentations until the time the plaintiff learned of the misrepresentations. A sex abuse victim who learns, years after his abuse, that a school acted to affirmatively cover up for a known sex abuser can claim that he relied on various "misrepresentations" which induced him to refrain from filing a

---

[59] 2013 WL 2120654, *21 (EDNY 2013).
[60] *Id.* (*citing, Harkin v. Culleton*, 156 A.D.2d 19, 23 (1st Dept. 1990) (fact issues precluded dismissal on statute of limitations basis in medical malpractice action))..
[61] *Bild*, 2013 WL 2120654 at *21 (emphasis added).
[62] *Id.* (Court invoked equitable estoppel in contract action where defendant lulled plaintiff into withholding suit through "affirmative misconduct" consisting of repeated misrepresentations).

lawsuit against the school and culpable school officials. These allegations will toll the statute of limitations. A plaintiff would then have three years to sue a school (and its culpable officials) for negligent retention and supervision after he learns of the school's misrepresentations.

Judge G.B. Smith, in his dissenting opinion in *Zumpano*, noted that for plaintiffs to show that defendants should be equitably estopped from asserting a statute of limitations bar, they must show "due diligence" in bringing the action.[63] Due diligence in this context means that "as soon as the plaintiff learns of the misrepresentation" he must seek to bring an action against defendant.[64]

Judge Smith's statement comports with well-settled New York law, which mandates that when the conduct relied upon is "fraud, misrepresentation, or other deception," a plaintiff must exercise due diligence[65] by filing suit "within a reasonable time

---

[63] 6 N.Y.3d at 683 (G.B. Smith, dissenting). The majority opinion in *Zumpano* also recognized that the time for plaintiffs to begin their investigation against a school began to run (meaning the tolled statute of limitation began to run anew) only after the facts giving rise to the estoppel—in their example, the alleged fiduciary relationship between student and school—ceased. *Id.* at 676. The *Zumpano* majority held that plaintiffs failed to plead any affirmative misrepresentations by the church defendants which occurred *after* the plaintiffs had been sexually abused, *Id.* at 674-75, so the majority opinion did not discuss whether the same rule would hold true if the facts giving rise to the estoppel were post-abuse affirmative representations. Nothing in *Zumpano* or, for that matter, New York jurisprudence, suggests that the rule would not hold true in that instance. *See also*, Chapter I.C-E, *supra.*

[64] *Id.*

[65] The use of the term "due diligence" is susceptible to confusion. When a defendant has engaged in post-abuse misrepresentations or affirmative misconduct which give rise to estoppel, the plaintiff in a school sex abuse case must exercise "due diligence" by filing a lawsuit within the statutory

after the facts giving rise to the estoppel have ceased to be operational."[66] Thus, a plaintiff's claims should be tolled until "the date plaintiff discovered the misrepresentation."[67]

Again, for a plaintiff to invoke equitable estoppel which is based upon misrepresentations, a plaintiff must demonstrate that she "commenced the action 'within a reasonable time after the facts giving rise to the estoppel have ceased to be   operational [,]' [meaning. . .] within the applicable limitations period as measured

---

limitations period, measured from the time when she learns of defendants' misrepresentations or affirmative misconduct. *See Zumpano*, 666 N.Y.2d at 676 (majority opinion) & 638 (G.B. Smith, dissenting); *Zimmerman*, 888 F. Supp.2d at 341. This does not mean that she needs to exercise "due diligence" by investigating potential fraud-based claims against defendants. Defendants' post-abuse conduct and misrepresentations which fraudulently led her to believe that defendants were not culpable with respect to her sexual abuse at the school should excuse her from that obligation. *See also, N.Y. Jur., Fraud & Deceit* § 176 at 247-48 (when matters are held to be exclusively within a defendant's knowledge, a plaintiff may reasonably rely on a defendant's misrepresentations *"without prosecuting an investigation,* as he has no independent means of ascertaining the truth") (emphasis added); *see also, Mallis v. Bankers Trust Co.*, 615 F.2d 68, 80 (2d Cir. 1980); *Swersky v. Dreyer and Taub*, 643 N.Y.S.2d 33, 36-37 (1st Dept. 1996); *Dimon Inc. v. Folium, Inc.*, 48 F. Supp.2d 259, 368 (SDNY 1999); *Patell Indus. Mach. Co. v. Toyoda Machinery U.S.A. Inc.*, 880 F. Supp. 96, 98 (NDNY 1995).

[66] *See Simucuski*, 44 N.Y.2d at 449-50 (motion to dismiss equitable estoppel defense denied where plaintiff filed suit within three years of her discovery of physician's false representations to her about effectiveness of medical treatment).

[67] *Bild v. Konig*, 2011 WL 666259, *5 (EDNY 2011); *see also, Commerce and Indus. Insur. Co. v. Imrex Co.*, 270 A.D.2d 147, 147 (1st Dept. 2000) (plaintiff must exercise due diligence in a commencing suit when a fraudulent misrepresentation intended to induce forbearance from suit ceases to be operational).

from the date plaintiff discovered the misrepresentation[.]"[68]

The "reasonable time" to bring such a claim after the discovery of a tolling misrepresentation is thus within the statutory limitation of the cause of action sued upon, measured from the date of plaintiff's discovery of the misrepresentation.[69]

Thus, if plaintiffs can plausibly plead that a school and/or its administrators or trustees made any misrepresentations to plaintiffs during their limitations periods which induced plaintiffs to refrain from commencing a legal action against the school, then plaintiffs can equitably toll the running of the statute of limitations on their causes of action for negligent retention and negligent supervision until the time plaintiffs learned of these misrepresentations.

---

[68] *Lipp v. Con Edison*, 158 Misc. 2d 633, 635-36 (Civil Ct., NYC 1993)(*citing, Simcuski*, 44 N.Y.2d at 449-50).

[69] *See Lazzaro v. Kelly*, 87 A.D.2d 975, 977 (4th Dept. 1982) ("[m]easured from the point at which the facts giving rise to the estoppel cease to be operational [e.g., upon plaintiffs' discovery of defendants' misrepresentations], plaintiffs' time in which to bring an action may not be extended for a period longer than provided for in the applicable Statute of Limitations"); *Niagara Mohawk Power Corp. v. Freed*, 265 A.D.2d 938, 939 (4th Dept. 1999) (where plaintiff alleged that defendants induced it to refrain from commencing an action by misrepresentations and active concealment, plaintiff set forth sufficient factual allegations of defendants' affirmative acts of deception to raise a triable issue of fact as to whether the doctrine of equitable estoppel should apply to toll the Statute of Limitations); *Zimmerman*, 888 F. Supp.2d at 341 ("in general, the length of the statute of limitations—measured from the time the basis for the estoppel ends—sets an outside limit on what will be regarded as due diligence") (internal citations omitted).

G.   *In Loco Parentis* Supervisory Standard for Schools: Representations from School Officials to Students Are the Equivalent of Communications from Parent to Child

In the school-student context, New York courts have specifically carved into the law a strict standard of care for schools and school administrators with respect to the retention or supervision of school employees. A school district thus "has the duty to exercise the same degree of care and supervision over the pupils under its control as a reasonably prudent parent would exercise under the same circumstances."[70] This heightened duty of care "derives from the fact that the school, once it takes over physical custody and control of the children, effectively takes the place of their parents and guardians."[71]

Accordingly, this *in loco parentis* "standard for determining whether this duty was breached is whether a parent of ordinary prudence placed in the identical situation and armed with the same information would invariably have provided greater supervision."[72]

The unique supervisory standard for schools should influence a court's assessment as to whether a school administrator's statement or conduct rises to the level of an affirmative misrepresentation to the extent necessary to equitably toll the applicable statute of limitations in a negligent supervision and/or retention case based upon the sexual abuse of a child by a school employee. By law, a representation to a child by a school administrator about an employee known to be a sex abuser must

---

[70] *Murray v. Research Foundation of State Univ. of New York*, 283 A.D.2d 995, 997 (4th Dept. 2001)(*citing, Mary KK. v. Jack LL.*, 203 A.D.2d 840, 841-42 (3d Dept. 1994).

[71] *Garcia v. City of New York*, 222 A.D.2d 192, 194 (1st Dept. 1996).

[72] *Murray*, 283 A.D.2d at 997; *Mary KK.*, 283 A.D.2d at 841-42.

be treated as if that representation was made by the child's own parent. This point has been entirely lost on New York state and federal courts, as well as litigants, which have adjudicated these kinds of cases.

In *Doe v. Kolko ("Kolko")*,[73] for instance, District Judge Townes dismissed two separate but related negligence cases filed by two alleged sex abuse victims against, *inter alia,* a Jewish day school where plaintiffs argued unsuccessfully that it was unnecessary for them "to allege misrepresentations or deceptive conduct directed specifically at them," but that representations made to the public at large or to a specific audience—in this case the local Jewish Community—were sufficient to trigger equitable estoppel.[74]

Plaintiffs in cases like *Kolko* should instead argue that pursuant to the applicable *in loco parentis* supervisory standard communications made by school officials to students should be treated by courts as if they were made with the immediacy and intimacy of a communication from parent to child. This should hold true whether a school official speaks directly to a student on a one-on-one basis or to a classroom (or even larger group) of students. In the latter instance, New York law provides that the school official is still the equivalent of a surrogate parent, albeit to a plethora of kids.[75]

---

[73] 2008 WL 4146199 (EDNY 2008).

[74] *Id.* at 4.

[75] *See Mirand v. City of New York*, 190 A.D.2d 282, 288 (1st Dept. 1993) (schools owe students a "special duty" which arises because a school that has taken physical custody over a child has deprived that student of the protection of his parents or guardian); *see also, Melzer v. Bd. of Educ. of City School Dist. of City of New York*, 336 F.3d 185, 199 (2d Cir. 2003) (school authority "acts in loco parentis for a group of students").

H.   Deception Through the Destruction of Records:
Another Potential Basis for Equitable Estoppel

Well-established New York law provides that a negligent retention and supervision claim in New York may be tolled if a plaintiff alleges "fraud, misrepresentation, or deception" which prevented him from filing suit.[76] The latter tolling mechanism, deception absent fraud or misrepresentation, has rarely been relied upon by plaintiffs seeking to assert equitable estoppel. If a plaintiff can allege deception in the form of a school's destruction or spoliation of records related to sexual abuse complaints or investigations, however, he may be able to assert this kind of deception as an independent basis for equitable tolling of negligent retention and supervision claims.

In *Anonymous v. High School for Environmental Studies*,[77] the First Department held that school records related to retention, supervision, discipline, termination, and complaints about, claims against, or investigations into a teacher accused of sexually abusing a student are "material and necessary to a fair resolution" of a student's action against the school for negligent supervision and retention.[78]

A school or school official, therefore, which destroys notes or investigative records pertaining to a teacher who allegedly sexually abused students has deprived a potential plaintiff of documents necessary for him to plead and prove negligent retention and supervision, and thus has arguably engaged in the requisite "deception" needed to trigger equitable estoppel.[79]

---

[76] *See Zumpano*, 666 N.Y.3d at 674 (*citing, Simcuski*, 44 N.Y.2d at 449).

[77] 32 A.D.2d 353 (1st Dept. 2006).

[78] *Id.* at 358.

[79] *See Kamruddin v. Desmond*, 293 A.D.2d 714, 715 (2d Dept. 2002) (medical providers' delay in producing medical records requested by patient

In *Kamruddin v. Desmond*, the fact that the medical malpractice claim was "under investigation despite [defendants'] intentional concealment [of records] [did] not preclude application of the doctrine of equitable estoppel. The determinative factor [was] whether there [was] a purposeful concealment."[80] So, in a school abuse case, if a plaintiff can prove that the defendants destroyed critical records—within his limitations period—he may invoke equitable estoppel on the basis of this deception.

The last element, the time in which the destruction of records occurred, is usually within the exclusive knowledge of defendants. That fact may thus be sufficiently pled on "information and belief."[81]

---

until day before statute of limitations expired equitably estopped medical providers from pleading statute of limitations as affirmative defense).

[80] *Id.* (citations omitted).

[81] *See Carr v. Equistar Offshore Ltd.*, 1995 WL 562178, *11 (SDNY 1995) ("when the facts at issue are within the exclusive knowledge of the defendants, allegations may be made upon information and belief"); *see also, Oy v. Rainin Instrument Co., Inc.*, 1997 WL 576008, *2 n.1 (SDNY 1997) (where information contained in documents is within exclusive knowledge of defendants, a plaintiff may plead fraud "on information and belief").

II. VIABLE ACTIONS BASED UPON PRE-ABUSE MISREPRESENTATIONS

The *Zimmerman* plaintiffs successfully alleged that misrepresentations by school officials which occurred *after* plaintiffs were sexually abused by the Poly Prep football coach raised an issue of fact as to whether their *prima facie* untimely negligent retention and supervision claims could be saved pursuant to equitable estoppel.[82]

A separate but related analysis is needed as to whether future plaintiffs in "old" sex abuse cases can assert misrepresentations by school officials which occurred *before* they were sexually abused by a school's teacher or coach as the bases for independent actions against schools and their culpable officials.

A. New York Law Recognizes the Existence of a Fraudulent Misrepresentation Claim When a Party Fails to Disclose the Existence of a Known Danger Where It Is Expected that Another Will Rely Upon the Appearance of Safety

Some sexual abuse survivors may allege plausibly that their school made affirmative fraudulent misrepresentations to them by failing to disclose to those students the existence of a known danger: a teacher or coach with a known propensity to sexually abuse children, against whom credible complaints of sexual abuse had previously been made. These allegations may form an independent tort for fraud.

---

[82] 888 F. Supp.2d at 340.

In *McGrath v. Dominican College*,[83] the Southern District of New York Court held that plaintiff—the administrator of a young woman who committed suicide after she claimed that she had been raped and that the school failed to adequately prosecute or punish her rapists—sufficiently pled a fraudulent inducement claim. Plaintiff alleged that the school had failed to disclose to prospective students various sexual assault complaints (which allegedly occurred on campus) of female students. The *McGrath* Court held that the school had a "distinct duty to disclose known unsafe conditions" and that its failure to do so was the "equivalent of a misrepresentation":

> In New York, a failure to disclose the existence of a known danger may be the equivalent of misrepresentation where it is to be expected that another will rely upon the appearance of safety.[84]

In *McGrath*, plaintiff pled a viable fraudulent inducement claim on these allegations: (1) several female students had been sexually assaulted on campus; (2) these attacks were reported to school administrators; (3) the school and its administrators failed to disclose any of these attacks; (4) information on sexual assaults on campus would have had an impact on the decision of prospective students, including decedent, to apply for admission and enroll as a student at the school; (5) the school defendants

---

[83] 672 F. Supp.2d 477, 491-92 (SDNY 2009).

[84] *Id.* at 492 (*citing, McKinney v. Bellevue Hosp.*, 183 A.D.2d 563, 565 (1st Dept. 1992)); Prosser, *Torts* § 33, at 179 (4th ed.); *see also, William L. Prosser, The Law of Torts*, § 108, at 714 (4th ed. 1971) ("The causal connection between the wrongful conduct and the resulting damage, takes in cases of misrepresentation, the form of inducement of the plaintiff to act, or to refrain from acting, to his detriment.").

intended to misrepresent the safety of the school's campus in order to induce students to enroll there; (6) decedent justifiably relied on this misrepresentation of campus safety when she decided to enroll and live on campus; and (7) was injured as a result.[85]

The *Restatement (Second) of Torts*, § 310, "Fraudulent Misrepresentations Causing Physical Harm," likewise provides that "one who by a fraudulent misrepresentation or nondisclosure of a fact that it is his duty to disclose causes physical harm to the person...of another who justifiably relies upon the misrepresentation, is subject to liability to the other." Several New York federal courts have cited this *Restatement* section with approval.[86] Likewise, Dean Prosser has stated:

> In many situations, a failure to disclose the existence of a known danger may be the equivalent of [an actionable] representation, where it is expected that another will rely upon the appearance of safety ... The 'something like fraud on the part of the giver' ... consists in permitting another to rely upon a tacit assurance of safety, when it is known that there is a danger.[87]

Despite the requirement that fraud be pled with particularity, "allegations may be based *on information and belief* when facts are peculiarly within the opposing party's

---

[85] *McGrath*, 672 F. Supp.2d at 491-92.

[86] *See In re Simon Litig.*, 211 F.R.D. 86, 139 (EDNY 2002); *Eastern Motion Express, Inc. v. a Maschmeijer, Jr., Inc.*, 141 F. Supp. 477, 486 (SDNY 1955) (careless words are actionable when a party moves in reliance upon the words).

[87] Prosser, *The Law of Torts*, § 33, at 179-80 (*cited with approval in Cariffe v. P/R Hoegh Cairn and M/V Cairn*, 830 F. Supp. 144, 147 (EDNY 1993)).

knowledge."[88] This rule was invoked by the *McGrath* Court, which held that plaintiff satisfied Rule 9(b) with allegations, pled only *upon information and belief*, that other sexual assaults had been reported to school officials but were deliberately concealed from prospective students (including plaintiff's daughter).[89]

In *McGrath*, the entire basis of these allegations pled upon "information and belief" was plaintiff's knowledge of her daughter's own alleged sexual assault (in May, 2006) and another sexual assault on campus (in April, 2006), and the school's alleged failure to adequately disclose, investigate, or follow up on those two alleged sexual assaults.[90] Judge Sweet nevertheless concluded that plaintiff's "allegations of [the schools's] prior knowledge of prior similar assaults *based on the knowledge and belief* arising out of [the school's] treatment of the April and May, 2006 assaults, "still satisfied the Rule 9(b) particularity requirement."[91]

McGrath, read in conjunction with *Restatement (Second) of Torts*, § 310, and Prosser, *The Law of Torts* § 33, provides potential plaintiffs with a compelling argument that a school made actionable fraudulent misrepresentations to them when it failed to disclose the existence of a known danger—a known child sex abuser—even though its students and their parents relied upon the appearance of safety at the school.

Such an action should allege that: (1) one or more students had previously been sexually abused on campus; (2) these sexual assaults were reported to one or more school administrators; (3) the school and its administrators failed to disclose any of these assaults to students or their parents; (4)

---

[88] *IUE AFL-CIO Pension Fund v. Herrmann*, 9 F.3d 1049, 1057 (2d. Cir. 1993) (emphasis added).
[89] *Id.* at 491 (*analyzing* Fed. R. Civ. Pro. 9(b))
[90] *Id.* at 491-92.
[91] *Id.* at 392 (emphasis added).

information on sexual assaults on campus would have had an impact on the decision of prospective students to apply for admission and enroll as a student at the school, and/or would have had an impact on the decision of current students to continue his or her education at the school; (5) the school defendants intended to misrepresent the safety of the school's campus, or the trustworthiness of a particular teacher or coach, in order to induce students to enroll, or continue their education, there; (6) the student justifiably relied on these misrepresentations of campus safety and faculty fitness and trustworthiness when she decided to enroll in the school or continue her education at the school; and (7) the student was injured—pursuant to her sexual assault—as a result.[92]

B.   Fraud Claims Against Schools and School Officials Who Cover Up Sexual Abuse at Schools Are Not Merely Incidental to Negligence Actions

This fraud theory is easily distinguishable from those cases where plaintiffs pled incidental fraud actions against their sexual abusers. In *Doe v. Roe*,[93] for instance, the Fourth Department concluded that even though the defendant, the alleged sexual abuser, may have facilitated access to plaintiff through fraudulent conduct, his sexual abuse of plaintiff—not *his* alleged fraud—gave rise to the injuries from which plaintiff sought recovery.[94]

In *Schmidt v. Bishop*,[95] similarly, the Southern District of New York Court held that the evidence failed to establish a fraud claim under New York law against a church pastor in connection

---

[92] *See McGrath*, 672 F. Supp.2d at 491-92.
[93] 192 A.D.2d 1089 (4th Dept. 1993).
[94] *Id.* at 1089.
[95] 779 F. Supp. 321 (SDNY 1991).

with his alleged sexual contact with a twelve year old girl during their counseling relationship.

The *Schmidt* Court disregarded the pastor's misrepresentation to the girl that their "relationship was special and acceptable in the eyes of the lord[,]" because plaintiff's injury —at the hands of her sex abuser (the pastor)—flowed mostly from the alleged criminal abuse perpetrated by the pastor.[96]

The genesis of the rule that a fraud case should be dismissed if it is incidental to sexual abuse allegations was discussed in *Coopersmith v. Gold*,[97] in which the Third Department dismissed a fraud action against a psychiatrist who had engaged in a sexual affair with his patient during his treatment of her.[98] Plaintiff filed, *inter alia*, both a malpractice and fraud case against the psychiatrist after he ended their affair.[99]

The Third Department held that plaintiff's malpractice claim was not time-barred as a matter of law because "defendant knew or should have known that her romantic feelings about him were borne out of [the psychological phenomenon known as] transference but that he falsely advised her that such was not the case in order to exploit her sexually."[100] Plaintiff also claimed that she was unable to appreciate the reality of her situation "and understand defendant's actions as malpractice until he ended their affair."[101] The *Coopersmith* Court held that plaintiff sufficiently invoked equitable estoppel on plaintiff's malpractice claim as a jury could reasonably conclude that the long delay and the institution of the legal proceeding was the result of defendant's affirmative wrongdoing (i.e., his false representations to her that

---

[96] *Id.* at 326.
[97] 172 A.D.2d 982 (3d Dept. 1991)
[98] *Id.* at 982-83.
[99] *Id.*
[100] *Id.* at 983.
[101] *Id.*

her romantic feelings towards him did not constitute "transference.").[102]

The *Coopersmith* Court held, however, that plaintiff's fraud action should have been dismissed: "the rule is well established that the concealment by a physician or failure to disclose *his own* malpractice does not give rise to a cause of action in a fraud or deceit separate from the customary malpractice action."[103] Thus, "[i]t is only when the alleged fraud occurs separately and subsequent to the alleged malpractice that a plaintiff is entitled to allege and prove a cause of action for intentional tort [.]"[104]

The *Coopersmith* rule is therefore clearly limited to those circumstances where a plaintiff attempts to plead negligence and fraud *against the same actor and for the same conduct*. A fraud claim against a school and its officials who conceal and cover-up their knowledge of sexual abuse stands on its own weight. Such an action is not merely "incidental" to a negligence or malpractice action.

The *Coopersmith* rule is vulnerable to distortion. In *Mars v. Diocese of Rochester*, [105] the Monroe County Supreme Court dismissed the complaint of ten adults who claimed that a priest had molested them decades earlier (from 1977 through 1986).[106] The *Mars* Court concluded that plaintiffs' fraud claim against the diocese which had employed the allegedly abusive priest was deficient because plaintiffs failed to allege any specific, pecuniary losses which were separate and distinct from the sexual abuse.[107]

---

[102] *Id.* (citations omitted).

[103] *Id.* at 984 (emphasis added) (*citing, Simcuski v. Saeli,* 44 N.Y.2d 442, 451-52 (1978)).

[104] *Id,* (citations omitted).

[105] 196 Misc. 2d 349 (Sup. Ct. Monroe Cty. 2003), *aff'd,* 6 A.D.3d 1120 (4th Dept. 2004).

[106] *Id.* at 350-52.

[107] *Id.*

Mars also misstated the law as follows: "[i]n order to sustain a cause of action for fraud separate from the claims of sexual abuse, the alleged fraud must occur separately and subsequent to the abuse, and then only where the fraud claim gives rise to damages separate and distinct from those flowing from the abuse."[108] *Mars* overlooked the critical fact that the *Coopersmith* rule—which prohibits a person from suing the same defendant for both negligence (malpractice) and fraud—governs only claims brought against the same actor for the same conduct.[109] From a logical and historical perspective, the notion that in the sex abuse context fraud cannot possibly occur until misconduct occurs *after* a person is sexually assaulted is absurd and antithetical to well-settled jurisprudence.

In a fraudulent misrepresentation which caused physical harm action, the school defendants' pre-abuse false representations to plaintiffs proximately caused plaintiffs' reasonably foreseeable injuries from the criminal acts of an intervening third party (the sex abuser). As the New York Court of Appeals concluded famously in *Nallan v. Helmsley-Spear, Inc.*,[110] in a related context, "the fact that the 'instrumentality' which

---

[108] *Id.* (*citing, Coopersmith*, 172 A.D.2d at 984, *Doe v. Rose*, 192 A.D.2d at 1089, *Schmidt*, 779 F. Supp. at 326).

[109] *See* notes 82-92, *supra*, and accompanying text. Nevertheless, as the fraud "incidental" rule is now so deeply engrained in the law, a plaintiff's attorney may sometimes need to concede this point as a tactical decision. If there are other important legal principles at play and in dispute, it might be prudent for a plaintiff's attorney to keep the fraud is not incidental to negligence argument in his pocket.

[110] 50 N.Y.2d 507 (1980). In *Nallan*, a man shot in the lobby of a building established a *prima facie* case of negligence against the owner of building because the victim was "lulled into a false sense of security" at the building and therefore "neglected to take the precautions he might otherwise have taken upon entering the building." *Id.* at 522.

produced the injury was the criminal conduct of a third person [does] not preclude a finding of 'proximate cause' if the intervening agency was itself a foreseeable hazard."[111]

That is precisely the scenario at play in a school sex abuse cover-up case.[112]

Under New York law, it is not necessary for the alleged fraudulent representation at issue to have been the exclusive cause of plaintiff's action or non-action which led to his harm.[113] It is sufficient that but for the representation plaintiff would not have acted or refrained from acting; that is, the representation was a substantial factor in inducing plaintiff to act or refrain from acting.[114] A representation may thus be actionable in fraud even if the statement was made with "reckless disregard of consequences," rather than "deliberate intention."[115] A misrepresentation, put another way, is a "legal cause" in a fraud action of "those pecuniary losses which are within the foreseeable risk of harm it creates."[116]

---

[111] *Id.* at 520-21(*citing, Restatement (Second) Torts*, §§ 302B, 449; Prosser, *The Law of Torts*, § 42, at 271-72).

[112] *See Golden Spread Council, Inc. # 562 of the Boy Scouts of America v. Akins*, 926 S.W.2d 287, 291 (Sup. Ct. Tx. 1996)("[C]omment e to Section 302B of the *Restatement (Second) of Torts* . . . recognizes that there may be liability "[w]here the actor has brought into contact or association with the other a person whom the actor knows or should know to be peculiarly likely to commit intentional misconduct, under circumstances which afford a peculiar opportunity or temptation for such misconduct." (*citing, Restatement (Second) of Torts*, § 302B, cmt. E, ¶ D)).

[113] *State Street Trust Co. v. Ernst*, 278 N.Y. 104, 112 (1938).

[114] *Id.; see also, N.Y. Pattern Jury Instructions* 3:20 [Intentional Torts, Fraud and Deceit] (West 2004).

[115] *Curiale v. Peat, Marwick, Mitchell & Co.*, 214 A.D.2d 16, 28 (1st Dept. 1995)(*citing, State Street Trust Co.*, 278 N.Y.2d at 112).

[116] *Restatement (Second) of Torts*, § 548A [Legal Cause of Pecuniary Harm], cmt. a (this fraud rule is analogous to the rules as "to legal causation

Again, therefore, a plaintiff in a school sex abuse cover-up case needs to plead and prove that he relied on various school officials' misrepresentations as to the school's safety (and faculty's trustworthiness) and acted (by enrolling at the school or staying at the school) or refrained from acting (by not leaving the school or enrolling at a different school). His sexual assault and resulting damages (i.e., psychological counseling fees) were losses within the foreseeable risk of harm created by the school officials when they misrepresented and concealed from students (and their parents) relevant facts about a known danger: a school employee who was a known sexual abuser of children.

One should look at what the reasonable reaction of students would be if a hypothetical school official told them and their parents the simple and unvarnished truth. "Class, Mr. Perpetrator, here, your new science teacher is a known child rapist, who has raped at least three former students that we know about." This example would certainly have spurred students (and their parents) to act and refrain from acting in myriad ways which would have removed students from the zone of foreseeable danger. Mr. Perpetrator's science class, at minimum, would no doubt have been empty.

The same hypothetical school official's deceit, in representing that Mr. Perpetrator is a well-regarded and trustworthy teacher and concealing his (the school official's) actual knowledge that multiple sexual abuse complaints have been made against that teacher, should give rise to a fraud action by any unsuspecting student who was lured into the school under such false pretenses and sexually assaulted by Mr. Perpetrator.[117]

---

of physical harm resulting from negligent conduct").
[117] *See McGrath*, 672 F. Supp.2d at 491-92; *see also, Zimmerman*, 888 F. Supp.2d at 340.

No litigant has ever made a nuanced fraudulent misrepresentation which caused physical harm argument against a school in any New York state or federal case which arose in the context of an alleged school cover-up of sexual abuse committed by a school employee. Nevertheless, the novelty of an independent fraudulent misrepresentation claim for survivors of sexual abuse committed by teachers or coaches at schools where school officials intentionally made false representations to its students (and their parents)[118] as to the safety of the school and the trustworthiness of a particular teacher or coach should not prevent a plaintiff's attorney—in the right circumstances—from making this claim.

Such a well-pled claim would also get the benefit of the discovery-diligence rule for fraud actions. Accrual of these kinds of sex abuse cover-up claims can thus be delayed until the material facts and underlying misrepresentations are revealed publicly.[119]

---

[118] *See Prestige Builder & Management LLC v. Safeco Insur. Co. of America*, 896 F. Supp.2d 198, 203-05 (EDNY 2012) (a scholarly opinion which holds that in New York the doctrine of third-party reliance operates as an exception to the normal justifiable reliance element of common law fraud. In New York, therefore, "the doctrine of third-party reliance permits a plaintiff to show that a third-party relied upon a misrepresentation by the defendant, which resulted in injury to the plaintiff.") (*citing, inter alia, Buxton Mfg. Co. v. Valiant Moving & Storage, Inc.*, 239 A.D.2d 452, 453-54 (2d Dept. 1997); *Ruffing v. Union Carbide Corp.*, 308 A.D.2d 526, 528 (2d Dept. 2003); *Desser v. Schatz*, 182 A.D.2d 478, 479-80 (1st Dept. 1992) ("[I]t is of no moment ... that the false representation was not made directly to plaintiff.").

[119] See CPLR § 213(8). *See also*, Chapter II.F, *infra*, for a more detailed discussion of the fraud discovery-diligence rule in New York State.

C.   New York Law Permits a Plaintiff to a Assert a Negligent Misrepresentation Claim Based on *Restatement (Second) of Torts*, § 311 Principles

In *Zimmerman*, Plaintiffs cited *Randi W. v. Monroe Joint Unified School District*[120] (a case decided by the California Supreme Court) extensively in their motion briefs,[121] and although the Court did not cite that case directly, its Decision adopted much of the *Randi W.* Court's reasoning.[122] *Randi W.*, which relied on the *Restatement (Second) of Torts*, § 311(1), may also serve as the predicate for an independent cause of action for negligent misrepresentation in a New York sex abuse case involving a school cover-up.

The *Restatement (Second) of Torts*, § 311(1), "Negligent Misrepresentation Involving Risk of Physical Harm," provides:

> One who negligently gives false information to another is subject to liability for physical harm caused by action taken by the other in reasonable reliance upon such information, where such harm results (a) to the other, or (b) to such third persons as the actor should expect to be put in peril by the action taken.

Randi W. and several cases in other jurisdictions have invoked this Restatement section to support facially viable negligent misrepresentation claims in the sexual abuse context. In *Randi W.*, the Supreme Court of California invoked Section

---

[120] 929 P.2d 582 (Ca. 1997).

[121] *See, e.g., Zimmerman*, Docket No. 1:09-cv-04586, "[Plaintiffs'] Supp. Memo. of Law in Opp. to the Poly Prep Defendants' Motion to Dismiss the Third Amended Complaint," dated May 7, 2012 (Document No. 255), at 11.

[122] *See Zimmerman*, 888 F. Supp.2d at 340.

311 of the *Restatement*, where various officials as different school districts gave gratuitous recommendations "containing unreserved and unconditional praise" of a former employee, despite their knowledge of complaints involving sexual misconduct at his prior employment.[123] The employee was subsequently hired as a vice principal where he was accused of sexually assaulting a thirteen year old student.[124] A unanimous court, in adopting Section 311 of the Restatement, held that the recommending school officials owed a duty of care to third-party students "not to misrepresent" the facts in describing the qualifications and character of a former employee, if making these misrepresentations would present a substantial, foreseeable risk of physical injury to third persons.[125] "[H]aving volunteered this information, defendants were obliged to complete the picture by disclosing material facts regarding charges and complaints of [the teacher's] sexual improprieties."[126]

Likewise, in *Davis v. Board of County Commissioners of Dona Ana County*,[127] the Court of Appeals of New Mexico, relying upon *Randi W.* and *Restatement (Second) of Torts*, § 311, held that when a county's law enforcement officers gave an employment reference for a former detention sergeant, the county owed a duty not to make negligent misrepresentations to the psychiatric hospital that hired him as a technician, and to a patient allegedly sexually assaulted by him, by omitting information regarding the county's investigation and disciplinary action against him for sexual abuse

---

[123] 929 P.2d at 584.

[124] *Id.* at 585.

[125] *Id.* at 591. *Randi W.* also adopted *Restatement (Second) of Torts*, § 310, "Fraudulent Misrepresentations." *Id.*

[126] *Id.* at 592 (*citing, Garcia v. Supreme Court*, 789 P.2d 960 (Sup. Ct. Ca. 1990)).

[127] 987 P.2d 1172 (Ct. App. N.M. 1999).

of women.[128] Plaintiff thus pled a viable negligence claim against the county because the positive misrepresentations about the former employee (which concealed information pertaining to the county's knowledge that this man had a propensity to sexually abuse women), created a substantial and foreseeable risk of physical harm to third persons.[129]

Similarly, in *Jane Doe-3 v. McLean County Unit District No. 5 Board of Directors*,[130] the Supreme Court of Illinois held that elementary school students who were sexually abused by a teacher brought a viable willful or wanton conduct action[131] against officials from a school district in which a teacher had previously taught where the school district had provided false information to district where the abusive teacher was employed at the time of the sexual abuse in question.[132]

Several New York federal courts have relied upon the *Restatement (Second) of Torts*, § 311, in holding negligent misrepresentation claims viable. In *Jurgens v. Poling Transp. Corp.*,[133] for instance, the Court held that "[a] party who negligently provides false information to another may be liable" for physical harm caused by action taken by another in reasonable reliance upon such information."[134] "Such liability may arise where harm results either to the person who receives the information or to "such third persons as the actor should expect to be put in peril

---

[128] *Id.* at 1179.

[129] *Id.*

[130] 973 N.E. 2d 880 (Sup. Ct. Ill. 2012).

[131] In Illinois, such an action requires plaintiffs to plead and prove the elements of negligence, as well as "a deliberate intention to harm or a conscious disregard of plaintiffs' welfare." *Jane Doe-3*, 973 N.E.2d at 890.

[132] *Id.* at 888-90.

[133] 113 F. Supp.2d 388 (EDNY 2000).

[134] *Id.* at 397-98 (*citing, Restatement (Second) Torts*, § 311(1)).

by the action taken."[135]

In *Jurgens,* an issue of fact existed, precluding summary judgment, on plaintiff's negligent misrepresentation claim which was based upon negligent representations made by the defendant which recommended a company to plaintiff to unload and transport a toxic product from a boat into a truck. Plaintiff asserted its negligent misrepresentation claim, which accused the recommending company of falsely representing to plaintiff that the transportation company had the necessary fire prevention equipment on board, after a fire occurred during transport.[136]

Likewise, in *Carter v. U.S.,*[137] a recent Eastern District case, the plaintiff, whose home was invaded by armed law enforcement officers after a United States Post Office employee provided them with incorrect information that a suspect lived there, brought an action against the United States under the Federal Tort Claims Act ("FTCA") [28 U.S.C. § 2671 *et seq.*]. Judge Block engaged in a detailed analysis of *Restatement (Second) of Torts,* § 311 as a basis for liability under New York law.

Carter noted that, as explained in the Commentary [Comment 1 to Section 311], "the duty to use care in conveying correct information extends to anyone who "undertakes to give information to another, and knows or should realize that the safety of the person of [sic] others may depend upon the accuracy of the information."[138] Judge Block also emphasized that the Court of Appeals of New York has cited Section 311 and its commentary with approval.[139]

---

[135] *Id.*
[136] *Id.*
[137] 725 F. Supp.2d 346 (EDNY 2010)("*Carter I*").
[138] *Id.* at 355.
[139] *Id.* (*citing, Heard v. City of New York,* 82 N.Y.2d 66, 75 (1993) (The determination of whether defendant, by negligent misrepresentation, breached a duty to plaintiff and proximately caused the injury turns on the

In August 2012, the Second Circuit Court of Appeals reversed *Carter*[140] to the extent that the District Court held that New York would recognize a duty running from one who negligently gives false information to another to *all* third persons that "the actor should expect to be put in peril."[141]

The Second Circuit emphasized that for a plaintiff to succeed in a FTCA action against the Government, she must establish that New York law allowed a similar claim for conduct by a private individual.[142]

The Second Circuit noted that the New York Court of Appeals recently declined to adopt a "new duty [ ] based on negligent initiation of a course of events with foreseeable harm," and concluded that "[t]his is simply not a prudent expansion of the law."[143] The Second Circuit thus declined to extend the reach

---

reasonableness of both parties' conduct. Defendant must have imparted the information under circumstances and in such a way that it would be reasonable to believe plaintiff will rely upon it; plaintiff must rely upon it in the reasonable belief that such reliance is warranted.) (*citing, Restatement (Second) Torts*, § 311, cmts b & c)).

[140] *Carter v. U.S.*, 494 Fed. Appx. 148 (2d Cir. 2012) (*reversing, in part, Carter v. U.S.* ("*Carter I*"), 725 F. Supp.2d 346, (EDNY 2010) and *Carter v. U.S.* ("*Carter II*"), 760 F. Supp.2d 281 (EDNY 2011) (District Court denied defendants' motion to alter or amend *Carter I* judgment)).

[141] *Id.* at 151.

[142] *Id.* at 150 (this is referred to as the "private analogue" requirement).

[143] *Id.* (*citing, Lauer v. City of New York*, 95 N.Y.2d 95, 104 (2000)). In *Lauer*, a city medical examiner performed an autopsy and prepared a police report which stated that the plaintiff's child's death was a homicide caused by "blunt injuries." 95 N.Y.2d at 98. Based on this report, the police began investigating the child's father for what they thought was a homicide. Weeks later, the medical examiner conducted a more detailed study and concluded that the child's death was not a homicide, but he failed to notify the police of his new conclusion. *Id.* The mistake was not discovered for more than a year. The plaintiff sued the medical examiner and New York

of a negligent misrepresentation claim based on Restatement §
311 principles where the plaintiff and defendant did not have a
"special relationship" giving rise to a duty of care for
defendant.[144]

For the reasons stated in Chapter II.D, *infra*, plaintiffs in a
school sex abuse cover-up case should have no trouble in
establishing the requisite "special relationship" between the
school and its students. In such a case—unlike in *Carter*—
plaintiffs will therefore not need to ask a court to recognize a
"new tort" in New York.[145]

As discussed at length in the next sub-chapter, the tort at
issue, negligent misrepresentation, is well-recognized in New
York.[146] So is the duty of school officials—pursuant to their
"special relationship" with students—to protect the children in
their charge.[147] Restatement § 311 principles, which have been
recognized by the New York Court of Appeals,[148] may thus be
properly applied in an appropriate school-student sex abuse case.

City for negligent infliction of emotional distress. *Id.* The Court of Appeals
dismissed that claim because the medical examiner did not owe a duty of
care to the plaintiff. The *Lauer* Court concluded that plaintiff's claim was
fatally deficient because no "special relationship" was created between the
plaintiff and medical examiner either by statute or the medical examiner's
conduct. *Id.* at 102-03.

[144] 48 Fed. Appx. at 150-51. The *Carter* plaintiff alleged that an employee
of the United States Postal Service "negligently provided inaccurate
information for law enforcement purposes that directly resulted in an
unlawful attempt by ATF officials to execute an arrest warrant at the
[p]laintiffs' residence." *See id.* at 149.

[145] *See id.* at 149 (the plaintiffs in *Carter* conceded at oral argument that, by
relying on Section 311, they were asking the court to recognize a "new tort"
never before recognized in New York.").

[146] *See* Chapter II.D, *infra*.

[147] *See* Chapter II.D, *infra*.

[148] *See Heard*, 82 N.Y.2d at 75.

One of the illustrations to *Restatement* Section 311 states that a person could be found liable for a negligent misrepresentation where he makes an incomplete disclosure thereby giving a false impression: "A has charge of B, a lunatic of violent tendencies. A advertises for a servant, and C applies for the employment. A informs C that B is insane, but negligently gives C the impression that B is not violent or dangerous. C accepts the employment, and is attacked and injured by B. A is subject to liability to C."[149]

A false impression given by a school official to a child about a known sexual predator, thereby explicitly or implicitly counseling a child to trust that predator, is far more egregious than the above *Restatement* illustration which gives rise to a viable negligent misrepresentation claim.

D.   New York Pleading Requirements for a Negligent Misrepresentation Claim

In New York, a claim for negligent misrepresentation which led, somewhat circuitously, to sexual abuse was rejected by the Appellate Division, Second Department, in *Cohen v. Wales*.[150] The appellate court affirmed dismissal of a claim brought against a school board for recommending a former teacher for a position as a grammar school teacher without disclosing that the teacher had been charged with sexual misconduct. The pleading was deficient because plaintiff — an infant plaintiff sexually abused by the teacher—was not able to claim the requisite "special relationship" between defendant and either the person who

---

[149] *See Isham v. PadiWorldwide Corp.*, 2008 WL 877126, *9 (D. Hawaii 2008).
[150] 133 A.D.2d 94 (2d Dept. 1987).

threatened harmful conduct or the foreseeable victim.[151]

In a case involving a negligent representation made by a school official to a student which proximately caused that student's sexual abuse at the hands of a school employee, the injured student should have no difficulty in pleading and proving the requisite "special relationship" between student and school for a viable negligent misrepresentation claim to lie. "The Court of Appeals has likened [such a] "special relationship," as that term is used in a negligence context, between a school and its students to the relationships between carriers and their passengers or innkeepers and their guests."[152]

In most circumstances where a school continues to retain an employee despite knowing that he has a propensity to sexually abuse children, a claim for negligent misrepresentation, pursuant to *Restatement of Torts (Second)*, § 311, may properly be asserted. An examination of the pleading requirements for a negligent misrepresentation cause of action in New York makes that clear.

In order to state a claim for negligent misrepresentation under New York law, a plaintiff must allege that: (1) defendant had a duty, as a result of a special relationship, to give correct information; (2) the defendant made a false representation that he should have known was incorrect; (3) the information supplied in the representation was known by the defendant to be desired by the plaintiff for a serious purpose; (4) the plaintiff intended to rely and act upon it; and (5) the plaintiff reasonably relied on it to his detriment.[153]

---

[151] *Id.* at 95. Thus, in *Cohen*, the claim for negligent misrepresentation was rejected for the same reason—the absence of the requisite "special relationship"— that the Second Circuit relied upon in *Carter*. *See Carter*, 494 Fed. Appx. at 150-51.

[152] *Mirand*, 190 A.D.2d at 288 (*citing, Pratt v. Robinson*, 39 N.Y.2d 554, 560 (1976)).

[153] *Manliguez v. Joseph*, 226 F. Supp.2d 377, 390 (EDNY 2002).

The requisite "special relationship" for a negligent misrepresentation arises when there is a duty of care between the parties. A duty of care may arise when: (1) there is actual privity of contract between the parties' relationship; (2) there is a relationship between the parties so close as to approach that of privity; (3) if the defendant has fiduciary obligations to the plaintiff;[154] or (4) defendant is otherwise in a special position of confidence and trust with the injured party such that reliance on the negligent misrepresentation is justified.[155]

Put another way, in New York, "[w]hether a special relationship exists between two parties is an issue of fact, to be governed by the weighing of three factors: In determining whether justifiable reliance exists in a particular case, a fact finder should consider whether the person making the representation held or appeared to hold unique or special expertise; whether a special relationship of trust or confidence existed between the parties; and whether the speaker was aware of the use to which the information would be put and supplied it for that purpose."[156]   Many plaintiffs who were sexually abused at schools as children should be able to successfully plead the existence of the requisite "special relationship" on numerous grounds: (1) as students, plaintiff had actual privity with the school as third-party beneficiaries of the contracts between their parents and the school (for tuition, etc.); (2) plaintiffs had a relationship approaching actual privity;[157] and (3) defendants had

---

[154] *See Ossining Union Free School District v. Anderson LaRocca Anderson*, 73 N.Y.2d 417, 424-25 (1989); *Schultz v. Sunlife Assurance Co. of Canada*, 2006 WL 681239, *5 (NDNY 2006); *Stewart v. Jackson & Nash*, 976 F.2d 86, 90 (2d Cir. 1990).

[155] *Kimmel v. Schaefer*, 89 N.Y.2d 257, 263-64 (1996).

[156] *Suez Equity Investors, L.P. v. Toronto-Dominion Bank*, 250 F.3d 87, 103 (2d Cir. 2001).

[157] *See Ossining Union*, 73 N.Y.2d at 425, for the definition of this element

a fiduciary relationship with plaintiffs, or otherwise were in a special position of confidence and trust, given their in *loco parentis* supervisory responsibilities towards the children in their care.

Many such plaintiffs should be able to assert viable negligent misrepresentation claims when schools and their culpable administrators and/or trustees covered up for sex abusers and thus created an unacceptable and substantial risk of physical harm to unsuspecting children. When a school's administrators knew that they had their students' trust and confidence regarding the safety of the campus and school personnel, and the school was aware that students and their parents relied on its alleged safety to enroll and continue in the school, the requisite "special relationship" between student and school existed. (The Court of Appeals, indeed, in a negligence analysis, has stated categorically that the requisite "special relationship" between schools and students exists).[158] Moreover, if uniformly positive representations about a known sexual predator were made to students directly, and their resulting injuries (from sexual abuse) were reasonably foreseeable, negligent misrepresentations as set forth in the *Restatement (Second) of Torts* § 311 should be actionable.[159]

Particularly given the heightened *in loco parentis* supervisory standard of care for schools, especially with respect to protecting students from sexual abuse, many plaintiffs should be able to raise an issue of fact as to whether a school's entirely positive representations about a known child molester (made directly to plaintiffs *before* they were sexually abused at the school) were not

---

(which is a somewhat circular reformulation of the other elements of the tort).

[158] *See Pratt*, 39 N.Y.2d at 560.

[159] These cases would not suffer from the pleading deficiency—lack of the requisite "special relationship"—which doomed plaintiff's negligent misrepresentation claim in *Cohen v. Wales*.

reasonable and thus constitute affirmative negligent misrepresentations pursuant to Section 311 of the Restatement. These negligent misrepresentations may thus form the root of independent tort claims.[160]

Similar representations made *after* a plaintiff's sexual abuse but within his statutory limitations period may likewise be used as a discrete basis for the invocation of equitable estoppel to equitably toll all of plaintiffs' *prima facie* untimely legal claims.[161]

---

[160] This legal theory is distinct from the rule that negligent misrepresentation claims may not be made "in the educational context" to challenge discretionary academic decisions. *See Moy v. Adelphi Univ.*, 866 F. Supp. 696, 706-07 (EDNY 1994) (a claim for educational malpractice is "not cognizable in New York"[;] "New York Courts hold that state and federal administrative agencies are better suited to evaluate the quality of education than the judicial system."); *Paladino v. Adelphi Univ.*, 89 A.D.2d 85, 91-92 (2d Dept. 1982) (a court may not challenge the discretionary decisions of educators concerning the curriculum, academic assessments as to a student's performance, and, *inter alia*, the quality of instruction); *Ansari v. New York Univ.*, 1997 WL 257473, *5 (SDNY 1997) (cases holding that New York law does not allow for a cause of action based on negligent misrepresentation in the educational context all "rely, to some extent, on the educational malpractice doctrine and the courts' reluctance to interfere in professional educational judgments"). When a court is not required to review discretionary academic decisions, but instead must examine representations which threatened the safety of children, a negligent misrepresentation claim against the school and its culpable officials should lie. *See Ansari*, 1997 WL 257473 at *5.

[161] *See* Chapter I.D-E, *supra. See also*, *Isham v. Padi Worldwide Corp.*, 2008 WL 877126, *9 (D. Hawaii 2008) ("Section 311 . . . compensates persons for physical injury and is not limited to information given in a business or professional capacity." [and] "Section 311 of the Restatement (Second) of Torts requires only that false information be given, not that a false statement be made." *Id.* at *6.

Seneca Insur. Co. v. Wilcock,[162] a Southern District of New York case, demonstrates how a viable negligent misrepresentation claim may be pled in the context of sexual abuse. There, defendant, an Arizona corporation, completed and submitted to plaintiff, an insurance company, an application for insurance coverage for Kid Express, an Arizona day-care center. Under the entry labeled "losses" in the application, defendant filled out the word "none." The insurance company then issued a general liability insurance policy to Kid Express.[163]

Subsequently, the parents of two Kid Express attendees made claims against the day-care center based on allegations of sexual abuse that had taken place after the insurance company issued its policy to Kid Express. The insurance company plaintiff alleged that during the litigation of those two claims it learned that, despite defendant's representation on the application form that the center had no losses at the time it submitted its insurance application, Kid Express had previously suffered losses resulting from allegations of sexual abuse.[164]

Plaintiff asserted a negligent misrepresentation claim against defendant. The *Seneca Insur. Co.* Court stated that to prevail on a negligent misrepresentation claim, a plaintiff must demonstrate that the defendant owed it a duty, due to a special relationship between the parties, to provide correct information; that it was foreseeable that plaintiff would reasonably rely upon this information; that defendant knew that the information was desired for a serious purpose; that plaintiff intended to rely on the information; and that it was reasonably foreseeable that the plaintiff would be injured if the information it received proved

---

[162] 2005 WL 2898460 (SDNY 2005).
[163] *Id.* at 1.
[164] *Id.*

false.[165] The reasonableness of plaintiff's reliance, moreover, "necessarily turns on context."[166]

The Court rejected defendant's argument that the term "losses" required Kid Express, or its carrier, to have money taken away from it. Rather, the evidence demonstrated that "a trier of fact could conclude that [plaintiff] understood the term ["losses"] to mean that Kid Express had no prior sexual-abuse history." Accordingly, the Court denied defendant's motion to dismiss plaintiff's negligent misrepresentation claim.[167]

A negligent misrepresentation claim asserted on behalf of a survivor of childhood sexual abuse against a school and its officials, administrations, or trustees who engaged in a cover-up of sexual misconduct at the school would require an examination into the reasonableness of plaintiff's reliance on the school's misrepresentations. Unlike in *Seneca Insur. Co.*, where the parties were both sophisticated businesses dealing at arms-length with the other, a school making representations to a child as to the safety of the school, or the exemplary and trustworthy character of a particular teacher or coach, is required to protect that child in the same manner as expected of the child's parents when they had custody and control of the child.[168]

So, the representations of the school officials, for the purposes of this tort, would be treated precisely as if made by a parent—armed with the same knowledge as the school officials— to his or her own child. This provides some "context" as to the "reasonableness" of a child sex abuse victim's reliance on his

---

[165] *Id.* at 6 (citations omitted).

[166] *Id.* at 8 (*citing, Emergent Capital Inv. Mgmt. LLC v. Stonepath Group, Inc.*, 343 F.3d 189, 195 (2d Cir. 2003)).

[167] *Id.* at 7-8.

[168] *See Restatement (Second) of Torts*, § 320, Comment B; Chapter I.G, *supra.*

school for accurate information about school safety and faculty trustworthiness. These hypothetical school claims involve more direct injuries, and more obvious and reasonable reliance on information tendered, than the above-cited cases in other jurisdictions which affirmed the viability of negligent misrepresentation actions based on false information provided pursuant to employment referrals.

Miller v. State of New York[169] is also instructive. In that case, the New York Court of Appeals reversed the Appellate Division and reinstated the trial judge's conclusion that plaintiff proved negligence against the State of New York after she sustained personal injuries at a state university when she was raped in her dormitory.[170] There, the Court held that the evidence was sufficient to sustain the trial court's finding that the school, by failing to provide locks on the outer doors of the dormitories, was negligent in failing to maintain the campus in a safe condition in the face of reasonably foreseeable criminal intrusion at the school.[171]

In a school sex abuse case, where the school had knowledge that one of its employees had a propensity to sexually assault children, the subsequent criminal sex assaults of other children entrusted to the school's care would be far more "reasonably foreseeable" than the unknown criminal intruder in *Miller* whose rape of a student led to a finding of liability against the school. A representation made by a school official that a school is safe, despite knowing that a sexual predator lurks behind the facade of a respectable and seemingly trustworthy teacher, is pernicious and should be actionable.

---

[169] 62 N.Y.2d 506 (1984).

[170] *Id.* at 510-11.

[171] *Id.* at 513.

In New York, if a plaintiff can plausibly allege a school cover-up, replete with pre-abuse misrepresentations or other fraud which prevented plaintiff from learning that the school knew of his abuser's sick predilections, that plaintiff may bring a negligent misrepresentation claim against his school and its duplicitous officials who provided him with false information, years, if not decades, after he was sexually abused as a child.

E.   "Shadow of Fraud" Allegations May Invoke the Fraud Statute of Limitations

A plaintiff who asserts viable negligent misrepresentation claims against a school, and/or its officials, which covered-up sexual abuse allegations through misrepresentations to students, may also plausibly argue that the applicable statute of limitations for fraud causes of action under CPLR § 213(8) should govern. Under that statute, claims of fraud must be brought within two years of the time the plaintiff discovered or could have discovered the fraud, or within six years of the time the fraud was committed, whichever is later.[172]

The general rule in New York is that the statute of limitations for fraud is only applicable "where there would be no injury but for the fraud." Thus, where allegations of fraud are only incidental to another cause of action, fraud statute of limitations may not be invoked.[173]

Despite this exacting standard, several New York federal courts have held that the fraud statute of limitations [CPLR §

---

[172] CPLR § 213(8); *Prohaska v. Sofamor, S.N.C.*, 138 F. Supp.2d 422, 434 (WDNY 2001).

[173] *Prohaska*, 138 F. Supp.2d at 434 (*citing, Seven-Up Bottling Co., Inc. v. Dow Chemical Co.*, 96 A.D.2d 1051, 1053 (2d Dept. 1983), *aff'd*, 61 N.Y.2d 828 (1984)).

213(8)] should apply to negligent misrepresentation claims which stand in the "shadow of fraud."[174]

In *Ambassador*, plaintiff pled negligent misrepresentation where defendant company allegedly misrepresented certain facts which caused a pest control company to refuse to pay a post-audit insurance premium.[175] The Southern District of New York Court held that because "the complaint depends on the acts of misrepresentation, be it negligent or intentional ... [plaintiff's] whole complaint sounds as fraud." Accordingly, as "New York courts [should] consider the essence ... of the complaint in determining the appropriate statute of limitations applicable to a cause of action," the *Ambassador* Court applied CPLR § 213(8) to plaintiff's negligent misrepresentation claims and held that they were not time-barred.[176]

In *Argo*, the Southern District of New York Court likewise looked to the "essence of the complaint" in finding that a negligent misrepresentation claim—based on allegations, *inter alia*, that a corporation misrepresented its intention to preserve the independence of corporate debtor's management—was governed by CPLR § 213 (8).[177] *Argo* concluded that the

---

[174] *See Ambassador Insur. Co. v. Euclid Svcs., Inc.*, 1984 WL 341, *4 (SDNY 1984); *Argo Comms. Corp. v. Centel Corp.*, 134 B.R. 776, 796 (SDNY Bktcy. 1991); *Fromer v. Vogel*, 50 F. Supp.2d 227, 242 (SDNY 1999).

[175] *Ambassador,* 1984 WL 341 at *4.

[176] *Id.* (*citing, Rockwell v. Ortho Pharm. Co.*, 510 F. Supp. 266, 269, (NDNY 1981); *Video Corp. of America v. Frederick Flatto Assocs., Inc.*, 58 N.Y.2d 1026 (1983); *Sears, Roebuck & Co. v. Enco Assocs., Inc.*, 43 N.Y.2d 389 (1977)). *Ambassador* held that were the charge of negligent misrepresentation viewed strictly in terms of negligence, that claim would be time-barred pursuant to a three year statute of limitations [CPLR § 214(4)]. *Id.* at n.7.

[177] *Argo*, 134 B.R. at 794.

plaintiff's allegations—which mirrored those contained in his fraudulent misrepresentation claim in the same action— "stand in the shadow of fraud." *Argo* took care to point out, though, that its holding was limited to "situations where negligent misrepresentation is alleged according to facts that also state a cause of action for fraud."[178]

In *Fromer*, the Court carefully examined the appropriate statute of limitations to apply to plaintiff's negligent misrepresentation claim arising from an alleged Ponzi scheme. *Fromer* cited numerous New York state and federal cases which came to divergent conclusions on this issue.[179]

In *Fromer*, Judge Scheindlin, relying on both *Ambassador* and *Argo*, again looked to the "essence of the complaint" to determine that CPLR § 213(8) was the proper statute of limitations for plaintiff's negligent misrepresentation claim.[180] In *Fromer*, too, plaintiff's negligent misrepresentation claim stood "in the shadow of fraud" and was therefore governed by the fraud statute of limitations.[181] The Court emphasized, however, that its

---

[178] *Id.* Likewise in *Argo*, "were the charge of negligent misrepresentation viewed strictly in terms of negligence, the claim would be time-barred by the three-year limitations period provided in CPLR § 214(4)." *Id.*

[179] *Fromer*, 50 F. Supp.2d at 242 (*citing, Asbeka Industries v. Travelers Indemnity Co.*, 831 F. Supp. 74, 80 (EDNY 1993) (applying six-year limitation period of CPLR § 213(1)); *Milin Pharmacy, Inc. v. Cash Register Sys., Inc.*, 173 A.D.2d 686, 687 (2d Dept. 1991) (applying CPLR § 213(1)); *Country World, Inc. v. Imperial Frozen Foods Co.*, 186 A.D.2d 781, 782 (2d Dept. 1992) (applying three-year limitation period of CPLR § 214 (4)); (5); *Ackerman v. National Property Analysts, Inc.*, 887 F. Supp. 494, 508 (SDNY 1992) (three year limitations period, *citing* CPLR § 214(4)); and *Fleet Factors Corp. v. Werblin*, 114 A.D.2d 996 (2d Dept. 1985)); *Argo*, 134 B.R. at 794-96).

[180] *Id.*

[181] *Id.*

holding was "limited to those instances where negligent misrepresentation is alleged according to facts that also state a cause of action for fraud."[182]

In a claim of negligent misrepresentation based on representations by school officials which proximately caused a student to be sexually abused by a teacher or coach, therefore, it is imperative for a plaintiff to allege both a claim for fraudulent misrepresentation[183] and negligent misrepresentation.[184] In the event a plaintiff pleads such viable claims, based on his reliance on, *inter alia*, representations pertaining to the safety of a school and/or the character and trustworthiness of a teacher or coach, his reliance may be based solely on representations that occurred *before* the actual sexual abuse acts. This will allow such a plaintiff to trigger the fraud statute of limitations (which may delay the accrual of his representation claims) *and* escape from the at times draconian equitable estoppel net of *Zumpano*, which requires a plaintiff to allege misrepresentations or other wrongful acts which occurred *after* the plaintiff had been sexually abused in order to invoke equitable estoppel.[185]

---

[182] *Id.*

[183] *See e.g.*, *McGrath*, 672 F. Supp.2d at 491-92; *see also*, Chapter II.A-B, *supra*.

[184] *See, e.g.*, *Randi W.*, 929 P.2d at 591; *see* also, Chapter II.C-D, *supra*.

[185] *See Zumpano*, 6 N.Y.3d at 674-75; *see* also, Chapter I.C, *supra*.

F.   The New York Discovery-Diligence Rule: The Legal Standard for Imputing Knowledge of Fraud

A plaintiff who alleges fraudulent misrepresentation and/or negligent misrepresentation which caused his or her sexual abuse must still navigate the fraud discovery-diligence rule, which holds that a claim sounding in fraud must be filed no later than two years from when the plaintiff discovered or could have discovered, through the exercise of due diligence, the fraud. [CPLR § 213(8)]. Likewise, any misrepresentations made by the school or school officials *after* a plaintiff was sexually abused may be relied upon by a plaintiff to prove that he or she could not have discovered the fraud earlier through the exercise of reasonable diligence.[186]

As a school sex abuse cover-up becomes more egregious, ranging in the continuum of wrongdoing from continued employment of a known sexually abusive teacher or coach, continued positive representations about a known sexually abusive teacher or coach, sham investigations of students' sexual abuse complaints, to categorical denials (therefore direct lies) to students and/or their parents about a known abuser's sexual abuse history, a plaintiff's task of demonstrating that reasonable diligence would not have revealed the fraud earlier becomes easier.

The application of a fraud statute of limitations for New York state law misrepresentation claims, for the reasons discussed below, makes it far more difficult for a defendant to dismiss these claims on a motion to dismiss or motion for summary judgment.

---

[186] The fraud analysis therefore overlaps an appropriate equitable estoppel analysis when a plaintiff alleges that her claim accrued but that defendants' post-abuse affirmative misrepresentations or misconduct caused her to refrain from filing a timely lawsuit.

In New York, the time when the plaintiffs are charged with a duty to investigate a possible fraud is when it is established "that they were possessed of knowledge of the facts sufficient to suggest to a person of ordinary intelligence the probability that he has been defrauded[.]"[187] "Mere suspicion" of fraud does not constitute a sufficient substitute for knowledge of the fraudulent act."[188]

New York courts have thus held that the time a plaintiff could, through the exercise of reasonable diligence, have discovered an alleged fraud, is the time from which it "conclusively appears that the plaintiff has knowledge of facts which would have caused him or her to inquire and discover the alleged fraud."[189]

New York law thus provides that in a fraud action a plaintiff is not on "inquiry notice" to the extent necessary to trigger the running of the fraud statute of limitations until a plaintiff was aware or should have been aware of enough facts

---

[187] *Azoy v. Fowler*, 57 A.D.2d 541, 541-42 (2d Dept. 1977) (only where it conclusively appears that plaintiff had knowledge of facts of that nature should complaint be dismissed); *see also, Watts v. Exxon Corp.*, 188 A.D.2d 74, 76 (3d Dept. 1993).

[188] *Gorelick v. Vorhand*, 83 A.D.3d 893, 894 (2d Dept. 2011) (Second Department reversed trial court's dismissal of fraud action); *see also, Sargiss v. Magarelli*, 12 N.Y.3d 527, 532 (2009) ("on the record before us it is unclear how plaintiff could have discovered the alleged fraud earlier than she did").

[189] *Baratta v. ABF Real Estate Co.*, 215 A.D.2d 518, 519 (2d Dept 1995); *Rattner v. York*, 174 A.D.2d 718, 721 (2d Dept. 1991) ("The [fraud statute of limitations] does not commence from the date that plaintiff has positive knowledge of the fraud, but from the date plaintiff becomes aware of enough operative facts so that with reasonable diligence he or she would have discovered the fraud."); *Stride Rite Children's Group, Inc. v. Siegel*, 269 A.D.2d 875, 876 (4th Dept. 2000) (plaintiff raised an issue of fact as to whether it could have discovered the subject fraud earlier).

such that he could have discovered the fraud with reasonable diligence.[190] A defendant also bears a "heavy burden" in establishing that the plaintiff in a fraud action "was on inquiry notice as a matter of law."[191] As such, "[i]nquiry notice exists only when uncontroverted evidence irrefutably demonstrates when plaintiff discovered or would have discovered the fraudulent conduct."[192]

In *Armstrong v. McAlpin*,[193] the Second Circuit, citing well-established New York law, set forth an objective standard for determining whether a potential claimant has enough information upon which to impute knowledge of fraud to him:

> Where the circumstances are such as to suggest to a person of ordinary intelligence the probability that he has been defrauded, a duty of inquiry arises, and *if he omits that inquiry when it would have developed the truth,* and shuts his eyes to the facts which call for investigation, knowledge of the fraud will be imputed to him.[194]

---

[190] *See Gonzales v. National Westminster Bank PLC*, 847 F. Supp.2d 567, 570 (SDNY 2012).

[191] *City of Syracuse v. Loomis Armored US, LLC*, 900 F. Supp.2d 274, 292 (NDNY 2012) (court denied defendant's motion to dismiss fraud action where defendant failed to establish that plaintiff should have been on inquiry notice of the alleged fraudulent conduct).

[192] *Nivram Corp. v. Harcourt Brace Jovanovich, Inc.*, 840 F. Supp. 243, 249 (SDNY 1993).

[193] 699 F.2d 79 (2d Cir. 1983).

[194] *Id.* at 88 (emphasis added; *quoting, Higgins v. Crouse*, 147 N.Y. 411, 416 (1895); *see also, Wollensak v. Reiher*, 115 U.S. 96, 99 (1885) ("the law imputes knowledge when opportunity and interest, combined with reasonable care, would necessarily impart it.").

The *Armstrong* qualifier—"*when [an inquiry] would have developed the truth*"—is the Rosetta Stone of a proper analysis of the imputation of fraud issue. Accordingly, only where the allegations in a complaint clearly show that a plaintiff possessed knowledge of facts imposing a duty to conduct an inquiry *which would have led him to discover the fraud*, do New York courts have a sufficient basis to impute knowledge of fraud to him.

New York law provides, as a general rule, that the issue of when a plaintiff, acting with reasonable diligence, could have discovered an alleged fraud, ordinarily needs to be decided by a finder of fact rather than on summary disposition.[195] Indeed, the Court of Appeals has stated that "[w]here it does not conclusively appear that a plaintiff had knowledge of facts from which the fraud could reasonably be inferred, a complaint should not be dismissed on motion and the question should be left to the trier of fact."[196]

G.   The United States Supreme Court Relaxes the Investigation Requirement in Fraud Cases

Several federal cases, in examining this precise issue pursuant to the federal discovery rule (which is similar to the New York discovery rule for fraud actions), provide substantial color to our analysis.[197]

In *Merck*, the Supreme Court held that a course of action for a private right of action for securities fraud accrues when the plaintiff actually discovers the facts constituting the violation, or when a reasonably diligent plaintiff would have discovered the

---

[195] *See Erbe v. Lincoln Worchester Trust Co.*, 3 N.Y.2d 321, 325-26 (1957); *Schmidt v. Mckay*, 555 F.2d 30, 37 (2d Cir. 1997).

[196] *Trepuk v. Frank*, 44 N.Y.2d 723, 725 (1978).

[197] *See Merck & Co., Inc. v. Reynolds*, 130 S. Ct. 1784 (2010); *TRW, Inc. v. Andrews*, 534 U.S. 19 (2001).

facts constituting the violation, regardless of whether the plaintiff actually conducted any investigation after being placed on "inquiry notice" of a potential claim.[198]

The *Merck* Court set forth a brief history of the federal discovery rule, which it described as a "doctrine that delays accrual of a cause of action until the plaintiff has discovered it."[199] "The rule arose in fraud cases as an exception to the general limitations rule that a cause of action accrues once a plaintiff has a 'complete and present cause of action.'"[200]

The Supreme Court, indeed, has "long ... recognized that something different was needed in the case of fraud, where a defendant's deceptive conduct may prevent a plaintiff from even knowing that he or she had been defrauded."[201] Otherwise, "the law which was designed to prevent fraud," could become "the means by which it is made successful and secure."[202] Thus, "where a plaintiff has been injured by fraud and remains in ignorance of it without any fault or want of diligence or care on his part, the bar of the statute does not begin to run until the fraud is discovered."[203]

For more than a century, in other words, courts have understood that "fraud is deemed to be discovered ... when, in

---

[198] *Merck*, 130 S. Ct. at 1798. The statute at issue, 28, U.S.C. § 1658(b)(1) provides that the limitations period does not begin to run until "discovery of the facts constituting the violation." The New York fraud discovery rule similarly provides that the statute of limitations for a fraud claim [CPLR § 213(8)] does not begin to run until a plaintiff has discovered or should have discovered "the facts of the fraud."

[199] *Id.* at 1793.

[200] *Id.* (citations omitted).

[201] *Id.*

[202] *Id.* at 1793-94 (*quoting, Bailey v. Glover*, 21 Wall. 342, 349, 22 L. Ed. 636 (1875)).

[203] *Id.* at 1794 (*citing, Holmberg v. Ambrecht*, 327 U.S. 392, 397 (1946)).

the exercise of reasonable diligence, it could have been discovered."[204]

The Supreme Court also noted that federal courts have applied the "discovery rule" to claims other than fraud.[205] Thus, treatise writers now describe the federal discovery rule as allowing a claim "to accrue when the litigant first knows or with due diligence should know facts that will form the basis for an action."[206]

In *Merck*, defendant argued that the limitations period should have begun to run at the point the plaintiffs were on "inquiry notice," which it defined as the point "at which a plaintiff possesses a quantum of information sufficiently suggestive of wrongdoing that he should conduct a further inquiry."[207] The defendant argued that, at minimum, the statute of limitations should run from the point of "inquiry notice" where the plaintiff fails to undertake any investigation once placed on "inquiry notice."[208]

The Supreme Court held, in a finding critical to our analysis of this issue in the school-student context, that the

---

[204] *Id.* (*citing, inter alia*, 2 H. Wood, *Limitation of Actions* § 276b (11), p. 1402 (4th ed. 1916); *Kirby v. Lake Shore & Michigan Southern R. Co.*, 120 U.S. 130, 138 (1887) (The rule "regard[s] the cause of action as having accrued at the time the fraud was or should have been discovered.").

[205] *Id.* (*citing*, 2 C. Corman, *Limitation of Actions*, §§ 11.1.2.1, 11.1.2.3, pp. 136-142, and nn. 6-13, 18-23 (1991 and 1993 Supp.)).

[206] *Id.* (*citing*, 2 Corman, § 11.1.1, at p. 134; 37 *Am. Jur. 2d, Fraud and Deceit* § 347, p. 354 (2001 and 2009 Supp.) (various formulations of "discovery" all provide that "in addition to actual knowledge of the fraud, once a reasonably diligent party is in a position that they should have sufficient knowledge or information to have actually discovered the fraud they are charged with discovery")).

[207] *Id.* at 1797. As explained in Chapter II.F, *supra*, New York law imposes a stricter standard for finding "inquiry notice" in a fraud action.

[208] *Id. at* 1797-98.

discovery of facts that put a plaintiff on "inquiry notice" does not automatically begin the running of the limitations period.[209]

The *Merck* Court could not reconcile defendant's accrual argument with the securities fraud statute at issue, which provides categorically that "discovery" of the facts, including "scienter," an element of the statutory claim, is the event that triggers the applicable limitations period for all plaintiffs.[210]

Accordingly, although the term "inquiry notice" is useful to the extent it identifies a time when the facts would have prompted a reasonably diligent plaintiff to begin investigation, "the limitations period does not begin to run until the plaintiff thereafter discovers or a reasonably diligent plaintiff would have discovered 'the facts constituting the violation' ... irrespective of whether the actual plaintiff undertook a reasonably diligent investigation."[211]

In *TRW Inc. v. Andrews*,[212] the Supreme Court analyzed the federal discovery rule in a claim brought under the Fair Credit Reporting Act ("FCRA"), 15 U.S.C. § 1681 e(a). The Court noted that the lower federal courts "generally apply a discovery accrual rule when a statute is silent on the issue."[213] In *TRW, Inc.*, the Supreme Court held that the general discovery rule did not apply to a FCRA case because that statute continued specific language as to when a claim based on an alleged violation of FCRA accrued.[214]

---

[209] *Id.* at 1798. This is potentially confusing because *Merck* conducted its analysis using the looser "inquiry notice" definition proposed by defendant, rather than the two-pronged definition used in New York. *See* Chapter II.F, *supra*.

[210] *Id.*

[211] *Id.*

[212] 534 U.S. 19 (2001).

[213] *Id.* at 27.

[214] *Id.* at 29-30.

The Supreme Court's analysis of the discovery rule, nonetheless, is highly relevant to the underlying issues raised in this book. The Supreme Court stated that if plaintiff were placed on "inquiry notice" against a credit reporting agency, based on a suspicious denial of credit, then "the discovery rule would trigger the limitations period at that point, *only if a reasonable person in her position would have learned of the injury in the exercise of due diligence.*"[215]

In *TRW, Inc.*, the Supreme Court also cited with approval the leading treatise on statute of limitations and accrual issues for a critical point: "*It is obviously unreasonable to charge the plaintiff with failure to search for the missing element of the cause of action if such element would not have been revealed by such search.*"[216]

Such a simple common-sense rule should likewise apply to any analysis under New York law as to whether a sex abuse plaintiff asserting a case alleging fraud (or fraudulent concealment) against a school and its culpable officials could have discovered the underlying fraud of the school through the exercise of reasonable diligence.

In *Zumpano*, the Court of Appeals imputed knowledge of *negligence* to plaintiffs, but it did not specifically impute knowledge of *fraud* to them.[217] To the contrary, *Zumpano* specifically held that plaintiffs had failed to allege any fraudulent acts committed by the church defendants, either before or after the sexually abusive acts of the various culpable priests.[218] The *Zumpano* Court emphasized that plaintiffs, based on their knowledge of the basic facts of their abuse, could have "at least investigated

---

[215] *Id.* at 30 (emphasis added) (*citing, Stone v. Williams*, 970 F.2d 1043, 1049 (2d Cir. 1992) ("The duty of inquiry having arisen, plaintiff is charged with whatever knowledge an inquiry would have revealed.").

[216] *Id.* (*quoting*, 2 C. Corman, *Limitation of Actions* § 11.1.6, p. 164 (1991)(emphasis added)).

[217] *Zumpano*, 6 N.Y.3d at 674-75.

[218] *Id.*

whether a basis for [actions against the dioceses] existed."[219] The *Zumpano* Court did not, however, state or even imply that plaintiffs' basic knowledge of their abuse suggested to them "the probability that they may have been defrauded" by the church defendants.

Zumpano's imputation of knowledge language assiduously avoids any mention or reference to fraud:

> Plaintiffs possessed timely knowledge of the actual misconduct in the relationship between the priests and their respective dioceses to make inquiry *and ascertain relevant facts* prior to the running of the statute of limitations.[220]

The *Zumpano* Court did not find that plaintiffs were on "inquiry notice" to the extent necessary to trigger the running of the fraud statute of limitations.[221] *Zumpano* thus avoided an analysis as to whether plaintiffs were aware of enough operative facts so that, with reasonable diligence, they would have discovered any *fraud* by the church defendants. Had the Court engaged in such an analysis, and identified any fraud, its proper conclusion, pursuant to the above-referenced New York general rule on the imputation of fraud, would have been to deny defendants' summary judgment motion and defer judgment on that issue to the trier of fact.[222]

---

[219] *Id.* at 674.
[220] *Id.* at 676.
[221] *See Gonzales*, 847 F. Supp.2d at 570.
[222] *See* Chapter II.F, *supra.*

H.   The "Scienter" Factor: In a Fraud Case a Plaintiff Will Not Be Deemed to Have "Discovered" a School Defendant's "Scienter" (Intent to Defraud) Unless a Reasonable Investigation Would Have Revealed It (Regardless of Whether Plaintiff Actually Conducted an Investigation)

In New York, fraud is a different species of tort than simple negligence.[223] It is axiomatic that a plaintiff pleading a fraud action must allege "scienter," meaning intent.[224] CPLR § 213(8) specifically delays accrual of a fraud claim until a plaintiff discovers or could have discovered "the facts constituting the fraud." This language parallels the statutory language examined by the Supreme Court in *Merck* for an alleged securities fraud— i.e., that statute's limitation period did not begin to run until "discovery of the facts constituting the violation."[225]

In New York, therefore, when a defendant has committed a fraud, the statute of limitations should not begin to run until the plaintiff thereafter discovers or a reasonably diligent plaintiff would have discovered the facts constituting the fraud, including scienter, "irrespective of whether the actual plaintiff undertook a reasonably diligent investigation."[226]

As fraud requires a plaintiff to plead and prove "scienter," meaning the requisite intent to defraud, a party—like a school— which engages in fraudulent conduct will not automatically admit to committing a fraud upon the first hint, or suspicion, or investigation, of its actions. It is not unreasonable to conclude

---

[223] *See Allen v. Westpoint-Pepperell, Inc.*, 11 F. Supp.2d 277, 284 (SDNY 1997).
[224] *Id.*
[225] 28 U.S.C. § 1658(b)(1).
[226] *See Merck*, 130 S. Ct. at 1797.

that a school may often take steps to conceal its own misconduct even (perhaps especially) after a victim comes forward and begins his own personal investigation of the school.

In *Valentini v. Citigroup, Inc.*,[227] District Judge Sand reviewed a claim brought by an investor which accused Citigroup, Inc. ("Citigroup") of securities fraud in violation of § 10 (b) of the Securities Exchange Act of 1934, 15 U.S.C. § 78; (b) and SEC Rule 10b-5, and also asserted a common law fraud claim under New York law.[228]

Valentini noted that the Second Circuit has held that a "plaintiff discovers" a particular fact when a plaintiff obtains or would have obtained sufficient information about that fact to adequately plead it in a complaint."[229] "With respect to scienter, this means a plaintiff must—or a reasonably diligent plaintiff would have—uncovered sufficient facts to 'giv[e] rise to a strong inference that the defendant acted with the required state of mind' such that 'it is at least as likely as not that the defendant acted with the relevant knowledge and intent.'"[230]

Valentini then noted that to state a claim for common law fraud in New York, "a plaintiff must show a material misrepresentation or omission of fact, made with knowledge of its falsity with scienter or an intent to defraud, upon which the

---

[227] 837 F. Supp.2d 304 (SDNY 2011).

[228] *Id.* at 311-12.

[229] *Id.* at 321 (*quoting, City of Pontiac Gen. Employees' Ret. Sys. v. MBIA, Inc.*, 637 F.3d 169, 175 (2d Cir. 2011)).

[230] *Id.* (*quoting, City of Pontiac Gen. Employees' Ret. Sys.*, 637 F.3d at 175; *in turn quoting Merck*, 130 S. Ct. at 1796). A "strong inference" of fraudulent intent may be established "either (a) by alleging facts to show that defendants had both motive and opportunity to commit fraud, or (b) by alleging facts that constitute strong circumstantial evidence of conscious misbehavior or recklessness." *Shields v. CityTrust Bancorp., Inc.*, 25 F.3d 1124, 1128 (2d Cir. 1994).

plaintiff reasonably relied, and that such reliance caused damage to the plaintiff."[231] "The elements of common law fraud are, therefore, essentially the same as those required to state a claim under Section 10(b) and Rule 10b-5."[232]

In a finding critical to our analysis, *Valentini* held that "[s]ince the pleading standards for Section 10(b) and Rule 10b-5 claims are the same as common law fraud standards, it follows that if one is dismissed, the other should be as well."[233] "*The converse is also true.*"[234]

Valentini denied defendants' motion to dismiss plaintiff's securities law fraud claims because—pursuant to *Merck*—even though the investor received "storm warnings" which should have induced him to begin investigating, defendant failed to establish that plaintiff learned or would have learned of facts establishing a strong inference of defendants' scienter (intent to defraud) more than two years prior to the filing of the complaint.[235] For the same reasons, without added explication, *Valentini* denied defendants' motion to dismiss plaintiff's common law fraud claim.[236]

Valentini demonstrates that the *Merck* rule—that a plaintiff will not be deemed to have "discovered" a defendant's "scienter" unless a reasonable investigation would have revealed such bad faith intent, regardless of whether plaintiff actually conducted an

---

[231] *Id.* at 325 (*citing, Dover Lt. v. A.B. Watley, Inc.*, 423 F. Supp.2d 303, 327 (SDNY 2006)).

[232] *Id.* (*citing, Pits, Ltd. v. American Express Bank Int'l*, 911 F. Supp. 710, 719 (SDNY 1996)).

[233] *Id.* (*citing, Fezzani v. Bear, Stearns & Co.*, 592 F. Supp.2d 410, 426 (SDNY 2008)).

[234] *Id.* (*citing, Jacquemnys v. Spartan Mullen Et Cie, S.A.*, 2011 WL 5920931, *9-10 (SDNY 2011) (emphasis added)).

[235] *Id.* at 322.

[236] *Id.* at 325.

investigation after being placed on notice of a defendant's possible fraud—[237] also applies to New York common law fraud actions.

This means that a plaintiff who plausibly alleges a fraud action in New York based on a school's demonstrable cover-up of sexual abuse should rarely have her fraud action dismissed at the pleading stage on timeliness grounds.

This is a critical point: in a fraud action under New York law (pursuant to the Supreme Court's reasoning in *Merck*), knowledge of a defendant's pre-abuse fraud should not automatically be imputed to a plaintiff who does not conduct an investigation or inquiry after her sexual abuse by a school employee. In the fraud context, rather, a court must examine on a case-by-case basis whether a sexually abused plaintiff would have learned of the school's fraudulent cover-up had she conducted an investigation after she was abused.

When an ongoing or prolonged fraud is plausibly alleged, then, it would be "obviously unreasonable [for a court] to charge the plaintiff with failure to search for the missing element of the cause of action if such element would not have been revealed by the search."[238] Using the *Merck* and *TRW, Inc.* imputation of fraud knowledge caveats, in a school sex abuse cover-up case where plaintiffs allege plausibly that they only recently learned of defendants' misrepresentations and/or fraud, a court will rarely be able to conclude, at the bare pleading stage, that it "conclusively appears that the plaintiff ha[d] knowledge of facts which would have caused him or her to inquire and discover the alleged fraud."[239]

---

[237] *See Merck*, 130 S. Ct. at 1796-97.

[238] *See TRW, Inc.*, 534 U.S. at 30 (*citing, C. Corman, Limitation of Actions* § 11.1.6, p. 164 (1991)).

[239] *See Baratta v. ABF Real Estate Co.*, 215 A.D.2d 518, 519 (2d Dept 1995); *Rattner v. York*, 174 A.D.2d 718, 721 (2d Dept. 1991); *see also,*

I. The "Inquiry Notice" Red Herring: A School's Post-Abuse Fraudulent Conduct Excuses a Sexual Abuse Plaintiff from Investigating Whether the School that Employed His Abuser Defrauded Him

In *Zumpano* the New York Court of Appeals refrained from using the loaded, and easily misunderstood term, "inquiry notice," despite holding that plaintiffs' knowledge of their abuse, the identity of their abuser, and the fact that the abuser had been employed by the defendant diocese, obligated plaintiffs to "make inquiry [and] ascertain the relevant facts" which may have established that the church defendants were negligent and in part responsible for plaintiffs' injuries.[240]

In *Zimmerman*, Judge Block correctly stated that in New York a cause of action accrues from the date of injury, even if a plaintiff is unaware that he has a cause of action against the defendant at the time of the injury: "[t]he rationale [for this accrual rule in negligence actions] is that the injury puts the putative plaintiff on inquiry notice and, therefore, charges him or her 'with responsibility for investigating, within the limitations period, all potential claims and potential defendants.'"[241] The

---

State Farm Mut. Auto. Ins. Co. v. Rabiner, 749 F. Supp.2d 94, 104 (EDNY 2010) (plaintiff argued that defendants knowingly misrepresented and concealed facts in order to prevent discovery of the alleged fraud; court held that plaintiff's allegations were "plausible," and noted that "[w]ithout discovery, the court cannot make the 'fact sensitive' determination of when this fraud could reasonably have been discovered.")(*citing, State Farm Mut. Auto. Ins. Co. v. Accurate Medical, P.C.*, 2007 WL 2908205, *2 (EDNY 2007) ("[D]efendants' argument that plaintiffs' [fraud] claims ... are barred by the statute of limitations necessarily assumes facts that are beyond the pleadings and have yet to be developed.").

[240] *Zumpano*, 6 N.Y.3d at 676.

[241] *Zimmerman*, 888 F. Supp.2d at 337 (*quoting, Doe v. Archdiocese of Wash.*, 114 Md. App. 169, 689 A.2d 634, 644 (Md. Ct. Spec. App. 1997).

Poly Prep defendants, in *Zimmerman*, ceased upon that language to argue that plaintiffs, as a matter of law, could not invoke equitable estoppel because "[each plaintiff] was aware of his injury (the abuse) and the source of his injury (the identity of his abuser and, by extension, the abuser's employer)."[242] Plaintiffs, according to the Poly Prep Defendants, were thus obligated to conduct and complete their inquiries as to the school's potential involvement in or responsibility for their sexual abuse, no later than when they turned twenty-one.[243]

The Poly Prep Defendants correctly asserted that to invoke equitable estoppel in New York a plaintiff must exercise due diligence within a reasonable time after the facts giving rise to the estoppel ceased to be operational.[244] But, the school erroneously asserted that the facts giving rise to the estoppel were "the incidents of abuse."[245] As New York law makes clear, however, and as Judge Block concluded correctly, when a defendant in a negligence case makes actionable misrepresentations to a plaintiff within the limitations period, those—the misrepresentations (shrouded in fraud)—are the facts giving rise to the estoppel.[246] *Doe v. Archdiocese of Washington*, the case cited by *Zimmerman* for the "inquiry notice" rationale behind the negligence accrual rule, lends support to the above conclusion. There, a man who alleged he had been abused by

---

[242] *See Zimmerman v. Poly Prep, CDS*, Case 1:09-CV-04586-FB-CLP (Document No. 323)("Memorandum of Law in Support of the Poly Prep Defendants' Motion for Reconsideration and/or Clarification of the Court's August 28, 2012 Memorandum and Order, dated September 11, 2012"), at 8).The *Zimmerman* case was resolved before plaintiffs submitted a brief in opposition to defendants' motion for reconsideration.

[243] *Id.*

[244] *Id.* at 11.

[245] *Id.* at 8.

[246] *See Zimmerman*, 888 F. Supp.2d at 341; *see also*, Chapter I.E-F, *supra*.

priests at his church in the early 1970s brought an action against, *inter alia*, the Archdiocese of Washington for negligence, negligent infliction of emotional distress and other theories.[247] The Court emphasized that plaintiff failed to allege that he was "kept in ignorance of his right of action by [any] fraud" of defendants, either before or after he was sexually abused.[248] The court suggested strongly that, had plaintiff alleged a fraudulent act by defendants which kept plaintiff in ignorance of his claims, the result would have been different.[249]

As previously discussed, when a plaintiff can plausibly plead an independent fraudulent misrepresentation action based upon defendants' fraudulent conduct *before* she was sexually abused, a court, with rare exception, should not impute knowledge of that fraud to the plaintiff on a motion to dismiss.[250]

For fraud actions, New York's two-pronged definition of "inquiry notice" provides that a plaintiff must have knowledge of enough operative facts so that a reasonable person would believe it was probable that he had been defrauded by defendants *and* that if he exercised due diligence he could have discovered the fraud.[251]

As the *Merck* Court illustrated, many jurisdictions, like New York, define "inquiry notice" for fraud purposes to mean the time when a plaintiff is aware of facts: (1) that would lead a

---

[247] 689 A.2d at 637-38.

[248] *Id.* at 644.

[249] *See id.* at 644-45 (negligence claims dismissed as time-barred).

[250] *See* Chapter II.F-H, *supra*.

[251] *See Gonzales v. National Westminster Bank PLC*, 847 F. Supp.2d 567, 570 (SDNY 2012); *see also, Baratta v. ABF Real Estate Co.*, 215 A.D.2d 518, 519 (2d Dept 1995); *Rattner v. York*, 174 A.D.2d 718, 721 (2d Dept. 1991); *Stride Rite Children's Group, Inc. v. Siegel*, 269 A.D.2d 875, 876 (4th Dept. 2000); *Azoy v. Fowler*, 57 A.D.2d 541, 541-42 (2d Dept. 1977); *Sargiss v. Magarelli*, 12 N.Y.3d 527, 532 (2009); *Pericon v. Ruck*, 56 A.D.3d 635, 363 (2d Dept. 2008).

reasonable person to investigate *and* (2) acquire knowledge of defendants' fraudulent acts.[252]

In fraud actions, therefore, the term "inquiry notice" under New York law comports neatly with the well-settled New York standard for imputing knowledge of defendants' fraud to plaintiffs.[253] Again, even when a plaintiff has a duty to inquire or investigate a particular defendant, fraud will not be imputed to her unless and until it conclusively appears that she would have discovered the fraud had she conducted an investigation (regardless of whether she in fact actually conducted any such investigation).[254]

1.   The Threshold Duty to Inquire as to *Fraud* is Not Easily Triggered

In *Zumpano* the Court of Appeals stated that plaintiffs "were . . . aware that the [offending] priests were employees of the dioceses and could have brought actions against the dioceses, or at least investigated whether a basis for such actions existed."[255] This statement was made, however, purely in the context of whether plaintiffs could have discovered a basis for their negligent

---

[252] *See Merck*, 130 S. Ct. at 1794-97 (*citing, inter alia, Fujisawa Pharmaceutical Co. v. Kapoor*, 115 F.3d 1332, 1335-36 (7th Cir. 1997) ("The facts constituting [inquiry] notice must be sufficien[t]… to incite the victim to investigate" and "to enable him to tie up any loose ends and complete the investigation in time to file a timely suit."); *Great Rivers Coop. of Southeastern Iowa v. Farmland Industries, Inc.*, 120 F.3d 893, 896 (8th Cir. 1997) ("inquiry notice exists when the victim was aware of facts that would lead a reasonable person to investigate and consequently acquire actual knowledge of defendant's actual misrepresentations.")).

[253] *See* Chapter II.F, *supra*.

[254] *See Merck*, 130 S. Ct. at 1797-98; *TRW, Inc.*, 534 U.S. at 30; *see also*, Chapter II.G-H, *supra*.

[255] *Zumpano*, 6 N.Y.3d at 674.

retention and supervision (and similar breach of fiduciary duty) claims against the church defendants. *Zumpano*, indeed, made clear that it could not identify any allegations of actionable fraud against the defendants.[256]

This is a critical distinction. A plaintiff can succeed on a negligent retention and supervision claim against a school (or a diocese) if he establishes, in addition to the basic elements of negligence, that, *inter alia*, the school (or diocese) had actual *or constructive* knowledge of its employee's propensity to sexually abuse children.[257] This means that the school (or diocese) is potentially liable if it knew *or should have known* that its employee was a sexual predator.

The negligence investigative scenario constructed by *Zumpano* does not assume that a school (extrapolated for our purposes) or diocese is acting in bad faith. To the contrary, *Zumpano's* suggestion that an investigation by plaintiffs would have permitted them to ascertain enough facts to bring timely claims against the church defendants[258] presumes the institutional employer's good faith (i.e., if asked about the sex abuser, defendants would have provided accurate information about what, if anything, they knew about his history of sexual abuse). Such a presumption, shaky in fact as it is to begin with, would certainly not hold true if a plaintiff can plead colorable facts which indicates that the school (or diocese) had acted with the requisite "scienter" (i.e., intent to defraud). That "scienter"—as discussed above—is a unique element for fraud, and it almost always involves a showing of bad faith and intentional

---

[256] *Id.* at 674-75.

[257] *See Dunahoo v. Hewlett-Packard Co.*, 2012 WL 178332, *3 (SDNY 2012); *Ehrens v. Lutheran Church*, 385 F.3d 232, 235 (2d Cir. 2004); n.13, *supra.*

[258] *Id.* at 674-75.

deception.[259]

The bare fact that a student was sexually abused by a teacher or coach should thus not trigger even the first prong of New York's "inquiry notice" standard for fraud, which provides that a person has a duty to begin an inquiry as to whether a defendant engaged in fraud if, and only if, she obtains sufficient information which *"equate[s] to the probability of fraud."*[260]

A contrary conclusion would hold, as a matter of law, that when a student is sexually abused by a teacher or coach, she then has sufficient information—without a scintilla of more evidence or data—to believe that it is *probable* (more likely than not) that her school and school officials engaged in a fraudulent cover-up that left her exposed and vulnerable to a person whom they knew (i.e., had actual knowledge) was a child rapist or sexual abuser.

Although school sex abuse cover-ups are, tragically, not uncommon, it would be an abominable decision, from both a legal and moral perspective, to make the rule in the preceding paragraph the new legal standard for schools accused of fraud-based sex abuse cover-ups. As New York law provides that school officials stand in an *in loco parentis* relationship with students,[261] they are held to the highest duty of care for the children entrusted to them.[262] Not the lowest.

---

[259] *See Gaidon v. Guardian Life Ins. Co. of America*, 94 N.Y.2d 330, 348 (1999) ("fraud has generally been defined by behavior involving intentional, false representations and other connotations of scienter such as willfulness, knowledge, design and bad faith[.]").

[260] *Teamsters Local 445 Freight Division Pension Fund v. Bombardier Inc.*, 2005 WL 2148919, *10 (SDNY 2005)(so-called "storm warnings" cited by defendants did not establish, as a matter of law, that plaintiff had inquiry notice of defendant's alleged fraud) (emphasis added); *see also, Azoy*, 57 A.D.2d at 541-42.

[261] *See* Chapter I.G, *supra.*

[262] The vast majority of educators, one would think and hope (and pray), would be vigilant in protecting children from being sexually abused by

Zumpano, again, does not shatter our analysis as to the necessary trigger point for a sex abuse victim's duty to inquire or investigate a school's potential fraud. The investigative rule for fraud is simply different than the investigative rule for negligence.

In *McIvor v. DiBenedetto*,[263] a medical malpractice action in which the defendant physician's patient died, the Second Department held that defendant was not equitably estopped from asserting the statute of limitations as an affirmative defense.[264] The Court noted that plaintiff could have obtained, upon request, the medical examiner's report which stated the cause of death.[265]

The Court emphasized, moreover, "that no allegations of specific misrepresentations made by [defendant] [were] found in the record."[266] In this negligence action, the *McIvor* Court—like in *Zumpano*—assumed the defendant's good faith and imputed knowledge to plaintiff due to her failure to make any inquiry. *McIvor* suggests strongly, however, that if defendant had engaged in *bad faith* by making post-treatment fraudulent "misrepresentations" to plaintiff, the equitable estoppel analysis and result would have been different.[267]

The necessary component of "scienter" or bad faith for fraud, which is missing from any negligence analysis (like in *Zumpano*), mandates that a sex abuse victim is not required to investigate the potential fraud of a school which employed her abuser until she obtains some information or evidence, beyond the facts of her own sexual abuse, that her school acted with fraudulent intent to protect her abuser and/or the name and

---

anyone, let alone a colleague or subordinate whom they know has these dangerous predilections.

[263] 121 A.D.2d 519 (2d Dept. 1986).

[264] *Id.* at 522.

[265] *Id.*

[266] *Id.*

[267] *See id.*; *see also*, *Doe v. Archdiocese of Washington*, 689 A.2d at 637-38.

reputation of the school, rather than to protect her physical and emotional well-being.

This means that a school that engages in a long-term fraudulent cover-up and concealment of a potential sex abuse scandal, by keeping a *known* sex predator employed at the school, and/or by failing to promptly notify students, former students, parents, and law enforcement officials, that its employee may have committed heinous criminal acts, cannot automatically get off the hook by hiding behind the applicable statutes of limitation.

A well-pled fraud claim, involving either pre-abuse or post-abuse (or both) fraudulent conduct or misrepresentations by school officials, and independent fraud actions or fraud allegations in the context of an equitable estoppel argument (or both), should blunt the edge of an "inquiry notice" sword before it can even be unsheathed.[268]

---

[268] In other words, if plaintiffs know no school-related facts other than that they were abused, the identity of their abuser, and the identity of the abuser's employer (i.e., their school), a court should conclude that they did not have an earlier duty to investigate any potential *fraud* of their school or school officials.

2.   **The Secondary Duty to Discover Fraud is Likewise Not Easily Found, as a Matter of Law, When a School Continues to Engage in Fraud and Concealment of the Operative Facts Which Give Rise to Its Own Potential Culpability**

As discussed above, New York law provides that the at times confusing terms "inquiry notice," "storm warnings," or their equivalent, do not automatically foreclose plaintiffs from invoking equitable estoppel to toll applicable statutes of limitations (for negligence claims and otherwise) if plaintiffs can plead post-abuse affirmative misrepresentations or other misconduct, upon which they reasonably relied, which caused them to refrain from filing a lawsuit against a school and culpable school officials.[269]

As discussed at length in Chapter II.F-H, *supra*, it should be difficult for a defendant to establish, as a matter of law, that plaintiffs would have uncovered fraudulent and concealing conduct related to a school's cover-up for a sexual predator had plaintiffs engaged in an investigation or inquiry of potential fraud at the school at which they were abused. As the Second Circuit recently pronounced, a court must keep in mind that "[w]hile hindsight [may] show[ ] that the fraud *could* have been discovered, that fact does not [necessarily] support the conclusion that, on reasonable inquiry, the fraud *would* have been discovered."[270]

New York law provides, moreover, that a plaintiff's failure to investigate will not preclude a finding of reasonable

---

[269] *See Zimmerman*, 888 F. Supp.2d at 341.

[270] *Cohen v. S.A.C.Trading Corp.*, 711 F.3d 353, 363 (2d Cir. 2013)(Second Circuit reversed Southern District of New York court and held that ex-wife's general awareness of ex-husband's concealment of income did not put her on "inquiry notice" of the fraud alleged in her complaint, for statute of limitations purposes)(emphasis in original).

reliance on misrepresentations where the facts allegedly misrepresented "are peculiarly within the defendant's knowledge [and plaintiff] has no independent means of ascertaining the truth."[271] In such a case, reasonable reliance may be found even "where the truth theoretically may have been discovered, though only with extraordinary effort or great difficulty."[272]

In a school sex abuse cover-up case, a plaintiff should plead that any school official who previously made a deceitful misrepresentation about a sexual predator would not necessarily be truthful if and when pressed with a specific inquiry about that sexual predator. If plaintiffs can argue that school officials were less than candid when actual inquiries or complaints about a suspect teacher were made, or that school officials rebuffed complainants or threatened them with reprisals should they persist with their complaints, then it will be even more difficult for school defendants to argue successfully that plaintiffs' alleged reliance on the actionable misrepresentations was not "reasonable."[273]

A plaintiff in a school sex abuse case who asserts affirmative misrepresentations by school officials *after* her sexual abuse should at minimum survive a motion to dismiss which argues that her reliance on the misrepresentations was not reasonable.[274]

---

[271] *Doehla v. Wathne Ltd., Inc.*, 1999 WL 566311, *13 (SDNY 1999) (*quoting, Mallis v. Bankers Trust Co.*, 615 F.2d 68, 80 (2d Cir. 1980)).

[272] *Id.* (*quoting, Dimon Inc. v. Foliu, Inc.*, 1999 WL 280427, *7 (SDNY 1999)).

[273] *See Swersky v. Dreyer and Traub*, 643 N.Y.S.2d 33, 37 (1st Dept. 1996) (rejecting argument that plaintiff's access to defendant's CEO negated reasonable reliance on misrepresentation where it was unclear from the record as to, *inter alia*, "how candid [the CEO] would have been with any information" that he had).

[274] *See Doehla*, 1999 WL 566311 at *12 (where the reasonableness of the

Where either pre-abuse or post-abuse allegations of fraud (or both) are pled in a school sex abuse cover-up case, the critical issue is not whether plaintiffs conducted an investigation against the school after they were sexually abused, but whether they would have uncovered defendants' fraud had they conducted such an investigation. The insertion of a viable and sufficiently detailed fraud allegation in a sex abuse cover-up case, particularly when the fraudulent conduct continues after the plaintiff's sexual abuse but within his limitations period, thus turns the central finding of *Zumpano* on its head.[275]

---

reliance depends upon factual determinations that are not plain from a review of the complaint and its attachments, a fraud claim should not be summarily dismissed on that ground); *Swersky*, 643 N.Y.S.2d at 37 (reversing lower court's grant of motion to dismiss; court held that issue of reasonable reliance "should not have been resolved as a matter of law"); *Breslin Realty Assocs. v. Park Investments, Ltd.*, 1991 WL 340576, *4 (EDNY 1991) ("whether it was possible for plaintiffs to ascertain whether the alleged misrepresentations were true or false and whether plaintiffs' reliance was reasonable or not are issues of fact that may not be resolved on a motion to dismiss"); *Giannetto v. Knee*, 82 A.D.3d 1043, 1044 (2d Dept. 2011) (plaintiff raised triable issue of fact as to whether dentist should be equitably estopped from raising statute of limitations defense in medical malpractice action where dentist allegedly tried to conceal his malpractice by knowingly misrepresenting patient's condition and performing unnecessary and ineffective follow-up procedure).
[275] *See Zumpano*, 6 N.Y.3d at 674-76.

3.　　*Merck* Shifts the Burden of Proof for Constructive Fraud to Defendants in Securities Fraud Cases

Generally, the statute of limitations is an affirmative defense on which defendants bear the burden of proof.[276] Prior to *Merck*, however, some district courts held that in a fraud case, a party seeking the safe harbor of the federal discovery rule had the threshold burden to establish sufficient facts to show when it should have known of (or discovered) the fraud.

In *Merck*, the New Jersey District Court, in holding that inquiry notice triggered the statute of limitations, placed the burden of proof as to when the alleged securities fraud could have been discovered on plaintiffs.[277] The district court found that the plaintiffs had failed to "show that they exercised reasonable diligence but nevertheless were unable to discover their injuries and thus found the complaint untimely.[278]

The Supreme Court, in *Merck*, rejected the district court's interpretation and application of the discovery rule, and recognized that the securities fraud statute at issue contained no indication that the limitations period can sometimes begin before discovery can take place.[279] The Court reviewed the evidence on the record and concluded that it did not "reveal facts indicating scienter" at any point more than two years prior to when the plaintiffs filed their suit.[280]

The *Merck* Court held that whether the defendant acted with the requisite state of mind is a "fact" for purposes of §1658(b)(1), so that limitations does not begin to run until the

---

[276] FRCP 8 (c)(1); *see also, Take Two Interactive Software, Inc. v. Brant*, 2010 WL 1257351, *4 (SDNY 2010).
[277] *In re Merck*, 483 F. Supp.2d 407, 418 (D.N.J. 2007)
[278] *Id.*
[279] *Merck*, 130 S. Ct. at 1796.
[280] *Id.* at 1799.

plaintiff discovered or should have discovered that element.[281] The Court held that to find the complaint timely, it:

> need only conclude that prior to two years before plaintiffs filed their suit, the plaintiffs did not discover, and *Merck has not shown that a reasonably diligent plaintiff would have discovered*, 'the facts constituting the violation.' In light of our interpretation of the statute, our holdings in respect to scienter, and our application of those holdings to the circumstances of this case, we must, and we do, reach that conclusion. Thus, the plaintiffs' suit is timely.

The Second Circuit courts which have discussed or cited *Merck* have not emphasized the impact of its shift of the burden of proof for constructive knowledge of fraud to defendants in securities fraud cases. The Northern District of Ohio Court, in *Hawaiian Ironworkers Amnesty Trust Fund v. Cole*,[282] however, recently engaged in an incisive analysis of that issue. That court concluded, for the reasons outlined above, that "[t]he [*Merck*] Court placed the burden of proving that a reasonably diligent plaintiff would have discovered the facts constituting the violation at a given time squarely on the shoulders of the defendant."

In *City of Pontiac Gen. Emps.' Ret. Sys. v. MBIA, Inc.*,[283] the Second Circuit, relying upon *Merck*, held that facts showing scienter are among those that constitute a securities fraud violation, and that a securities fraud statute of limitations "cannot begin to run until the plaintiff discovers—or a reasonably diligent plaintiff would have discovered—the facts constituting scienter,"

---

[281] *Id.*

[282] 2011 WL 1257756, *14-16 (N.D. Ohio 2011).

[283] 637 F. 3d 169 (2d Cir. 2011).

which it defines as "a mental state embracing intent to deceive, manipulate, or defraud."[284]

The *City of Pontiac* Court refined the appropriate standard needed to assess how much information a reasonably diligent investor must have about the facts constituting a securities fraud violation "before those facts are deemed 'discovered' and the statute of limitations begins to run."[285]

The Second Circuit noted that because *Merck* specifically referenced pleading requirements when discussing the limitations trigger the *Merck* Court "thought about the requirements for 'discovering' a fact in terms of what was required to adequately plead that fact and survive a motion to dismiss."[286]

The *City of Pontiac* Court also looked for guidance from the basic purpose of a statute of limitations. "In contrast to a statute of repose, a statute of limitations is intended to prevent plaintiffs from unfairly surprising defendants by resurrecting stale claims. A statute of limitations prevents such surprises by extinguishing a plaintiff's remedy after he has slept on his claim for a prolonged period of time, failing 'to bring suit within a specific period of time after his claim accrued.'"[287]

The Second Circuit reasoned that since the purpose is to prevent stale claims, "it would make no sense for a statute of limitations to begin to run before the plaintiff even has a claim. Accordingly, [a] claim that has not yet accrued could never be considered stale." Thus, "in the limitations context, it makes sense to link the standard for 'discovering' the facts of a violation to the plaintiff's ability to make out or plead that violation. Only after a plaintiff can adequately plead his claim can that claim be

---

[284] *Id.* at 174.
[285] *Id.*
[286] *Id.* at 175.
[287] *Id.* at 174-75.

said to have accrued, and only after a claim has accrued can a statute of limitations on that claim begin to run."[288]

Based on this analysis, the Second Circuit held that "a fact is not deemed 'discovered' until a reasonably diligent plaintiff would have sufficient information about that fact to adequately plead it in a complaint. In other words, the reasonably diligent plaintiff has not 'discovered' one of the facts constituting a securities fraud violation until he can plead the facts with sufficient detail and particularity to survive a Rule 12(b)(6) motion to dismiss.[289]

---

[288] *Id.* at 175.
[289] *Id.*

4.   New York Law Provides that Where Plaintiffs
        Plausibly Allege that They Could Not Have
        Discovered Fraud Earlier, Defendants Now Have
        the Burden of Proving that—Had Plaintiffs
        Exercised Reasonable Diligence—Plaintiffs Would
        Have Discovered Defendants' Fraud Prior to Two
        Years of the Commencement of the Action

Under New York law, the burden of proving the affirmative defense of the statute of limitations rests on the party invoking it.[290] It is axiomatic, therefore, that the party seeking the benefit of the statute of limitations defense bears the burden of establishing by *prima facie* proof that the statute of limitations has elapsed.[291] To make a *prima facie* showing that the plaintiff's time to sue has expired, the defendant must establish when the plaintiff's cause of action accrued.[292]

Where a defendant shows a cause of action is on its face barred by the statute of limitations, the plaintiff must then come forward with some evidentiary facts showing that an exception exists or that the action is otherwise not time-barred.[293]

In the fraud context, this is a critical issue. Especially at the pleading stage, the burden of proof is essential. Does the

---

[290] *Carmody-Wait 2d*, § 13;522, "Burden of Proof" (*citing, Katz v. Goodyear Tire and Rubber Co.*, 737 F.2d 238, 243 (2d Cir. 1984) (applying New York law); *In re Rodken*, 270 A.D.2d 784, 785 (3d Dept. 2000); *Brush v. Olivo*, 81 A.D.2d 852, 853 (2d Dept. 1981)).
[291] *Id.* (*citing, Quantum Health Resources v. De Buono*, 273 A.D.2d 730, 730 (3d Dept. 2010); *Brothers v. Florence*, 262 A.D.2d 261, 262 (2d Dept. 1999), *aff'd on other grounds*, 95 N.Y.2d 290 (2000)).
[292] *In re Schwartz*, 44 A.D.3d 779, 779 (2d Dept. 2007); *Swift v. New York Medical College*, 25 A.D.3d 686, 687 (2d Dept. 2006).
[293] *Texeria v. BAB Nuclear Radiology*, 43 A.D.3d 403, 405 (2d Dept. 2007).

plaintiff need to establish evidentiary facts that the alleged fraud could not have been discovered before the two year period [as set forth in CPLR § 213(8)] prior to the commencement of the action? Or does the defendant need to aver facts which demonstrate that plaintiff could have discovered the facts earlier than two years prior to the commencement of the action?

Prior to 2009, New York courts frequently held that a plaintiff who sought "the benefit of the discovery exception to the six year statute of limitations for fraud had the burden of establishing that the fraud could not have been discovered before the two-year period prior to the commencement of the action."[294]

These courts treated the fraud discovery rule, as set forth in CPLR § 203(g) and (in 2004) memorialized in CPLR § 213(8), as an exception to the standard fraud accrual rule [6 years pursuant to CPLR § 213(8)], rather than an independent fraud accrual rule. The following statement (or a close variation) thus appears in several dozen New York state and federal cases: "[a]n action based upon fraud must be commenced within the greater of 6 years from the date the cause of action accrued or 2 years from the time plaintiff discovered or, with reasonable diligence, could have discovered the fraud."[295]

That statement, as ubiquitous as it is in the New York law books[296] is simply wrong, and misconstrues the fraud accrual rule.

In the 1950s, the New York Civil Practice Act, § 48, Subd. 5, provided a six-year period of limitations as to actions for fraud, a period which began to run only from the discovery of the

---

[294] *See Von Blomberg v. Garis*, 44 A.D.3d 1033, 1034 (2d Dept. 2007); *Siler v. Lutheran Soc. Servs. of Metro. N.Y.*, 10 A.D.3d 646, 648 (2d Dept. 2004); *Lefkowitz v. Applebaum*, 258 A.D.2d 563 (2d Dept. 1999).
[295] *See, e.g., Gutkin v. Siegal*, 85 A.D.3d 687, 687 (1st Dept. 2011).
[296] At least twenty-seven state courts and eighteen federal courts have cited that statement with approval.

fraud."[297] Accordingly, "[t]he cause of action in [a fraud] case [was] not deemed to have accrued until the discovery by the plaintiff of the facts constituting the fraud[.]" [Civil Practice Act, § 48, Subd. 5, compiled in, 8 Gilbert–Bliss Civil Practice of the State of New York 13 (1956); *see also, Erbe v. Lincoln Rochester Trust Co.*, 3 N.Y.2d 321, 326 (1957)].

In 1965, New York enacted the predecessor of what is now N.Y. CPLR § 203(g).[298] That section now provides, with limited exceptions, that "where the time within which an action must be commenced is computed from the time when facts were discovered or from the time when facts could with reasonable diligence could have been discovered,… the action must be commenced within two years after such actual or imputed discovery or within the period otherwise provided, *computed from the time the cause of action accrued, whichever is longer.*"[299] (emphasis added). CPLR § 203(g) itself thus provides that the longer period after when "the cause of action accrued" —*either* six years after the fraud occurred *or* two years after the fraud was or could (with reasonable diligence) have been discovered— is the outside date on which the fraud statute of limitations expires.

Any ambiguity as to whether the fraud discovery rule is an independent accrual rule (which it is) or an exception to the fraud accrual rule (which, contrary to popular belief, it is not) was put to rest in 2004, when CPLR § 213(8), the limitations period for fraud-based actions, was amended to include explicitly the two year discovery limitation of CPLR § 203(g).[300]

---

[297] *Rieser v. Balt. & Ohio R.R. Co.*, 228 F.2d 563, 566 (2d Cir. 1955).

[298] *See* 1965 N.Y. Laws 56.

[299] N.Y. CPLR § 203(g) (McKinney 2001).

[300] *See Koch v. Christie's Int'l PLC*, 699 F.3d 141, 154 n.6 (2d Cir. 2012) (*citing*, 1 Weinstein, Korn & Miller, New York Civil Practice: CPLR ¶¶ 203. App. 03, 203, 35, 213 App. 01, 213 App. 03).

A fraud which was concealed for more than six years thus *accrues* only when a plaintiff discovers or could have discovered (through reasonable diligence) the facts constituting that fraud.

But old (and bad) habits die hard. In 2008, the Appellate Division, Second Department, in *Sargiss v. Magarelli*,[301] granted defendant's motion to dismiss a fraud claim as untimely where the action was commenced more than six years after the alleged fraud, and the plaintiff "failed to satisfy her burden of establishing that the fraud could not have been discovered prior to the two-year period before the commencement of the action."[302] The Second Department held, again, that "[t]he burden of establishing that the fraud could not have been discovered prior to the two-year period before the commencement of the action *rests on the plaintiff who seeks the benefit of the exception*." *Id.* (citations omitted; emphasis added).

The Court of Appeals, in *Sargiss*, held that the trial court erred in granting the defendant's motion to dismiss plaintiff's fraud action[303] because the defendant failed to demonstrate that plaintiff could have discovered his fraud earlier with reasonable diligence.[304] Although the Court of Appeals did not definitively state that it was reversing the concealed fraud burden of proof rule, two Second Department courts have interpreted *Sargiss* to stand for such a rule: when a plaintiff alleges that he has commenced an action within two years of his discovery of fraud, it is then *defendant's* burden to demonstrate, *prima facie*, that the fraud could have been discovered earlier with reasonable diligence.[305] This proper analysis comports with the above rule

---

[301] 50 A.D.3d 1117, 1118 (2d Dept. 2008).

[302] *Id.* at 1118.

[303] 12 N.Y.3d 527, 532 (2009).

[304] *Id.* at 532.

[305] *Vilsack v. Meyer*, 96 A.D.3d 827, 829 (2d Dept. 2013); *House of Spices (India) Inc. v. SMJ Services, Inc.*, 103 A.D.3d 848, 849 (2d Dept.

that a concealed fraud does not *accrue* until a plaintiff discovers or could have discovered the underlying fraud facts.

J.   Emotional Distress and Pain and Suffering Damages

Damages for emotional distress and pain and suffering are not recoverable for fraud actions.[306] If, however, plaintiffs are able to establish that they suffered some pecuniary injury, successful fraud plaintiffs can recover their out-of-pocket pecuniary losses at trial.[307] Plaintiffs in these cases must plead and prove that they incurred out-of-pocket losses, such as, for instance, fees for psychological treatment and/or counseling, which were directly related to the sexual abuse that they suffered at school.

As plaintiffs in school sexual abuse cases will have actually suffered physical harm (their sexual assaults), as well as emotional injuries, a plaintiff who pleads and proves a Section 311 negligent misrepresentation claim against a school and its culpable officials is entitled to recover compensatory damages for her emotional distress and pain and suffering. As the principal goal of a Section 311 negligent misrepresentation claim is to "compensate persons for their injuries,"[308] it follows that

---

2013).

[306] *Jeffrey "BB" v. Cardinal McCloskey School and Home for Children*, 257 A.D.2d 21, 24 (3d Dept. 1999) (Third Department reversed trial court order on fraud claim stemming from allegations that child placement agency had concealed from adoptive parents the fact that a child placed in adoptive home had been a victim of sexual abuse; issues of material fact as to concealment, materiality, causal connection, and scienter, precluded summary judgment for defendants).

[307] *Id.*; *see also, Weissman v. Dow Corning Corp.*, 892 F. Supp. 510, 515 (SDNY 1995)(damages available for fraud do not include pain and suffering [but] a fraud claim may encompass some damages that stem from personal injuries").

[308] *Isham*, 2008 WL 877126 at *9.

damages for pain and suffering and emotional distress which flow directly from those injuries should be recoverable for prevailing plaintiffs.

Along these lines, in *Alice D. v. William M.*,[309] the Court held that a claimant, who sought to recover on the basis of negligent misrepresentation after she became pregnant when defendant informed her—prior to engaging in sexual intercourse with her—that he was sterile, was entitled to damages for pain and suffering.[310] In *Alice B.*, the claimant pled fraudulent misrepresentation as well as a negligent misrepresentation, but the former claim was dismissed for failure to prove defendant's state of mind when he made the representation at issue.[311]

K.   Punitive Damages

In any event, plaintiffs should also plead punitive damages for their misrepresentation claims. As the New York Court of Appeals held in *Giblin v. Murphy*,[312] punitive damages are allowed in tort cases—even if there is no harm aimed at the public generally—where a "very high threshold of moral culpability is satisfied."[313]

Punitive damages are thus available to plaintiffs "where a wrong is aggravated by recklessness or willfulness,"[314] or where a defendant's conduct evinces "a high degree of moral turpitude

---

[309] 113 Misc. 2d 940 (N.Y. Cty. Small Claims, Harlem 1982).

[310] *Id.* at 949.

[311] *Id.* at 945.

[312] 73 N.Y.2d 769 (1988).

[313] *Id.* at 772. In school sex abuse cover-up cases, moreover, plaintiffs can claim that defendants' acts and/or omissions had a direct and profound impact on the public-at-large.

[314] *Roy Export Co. v. Columbia Broadcasting System*, 672 F.2d 1095, 1106 (2d Cir. 1982), *cert. denied*, 459 U.S. 826 (1982).

and demonstrate[s] such wanton dishonesty as to imply a criminal indifference to civil obligations."[315]

When a school official—entrusted with the duty to treat a child as if he or she were his own son or daughter—falsely represents to the child and her parents that a school is safe, and a teacher trustworthy, when he knows that the teacher is in fact a child rapist or molester,[316] that conduct surely evinces the necessary "moral culpability" envisioned by *Giblin.*

Under these circumstances, therefore, plaintiffs with viable misrepresentation claims based on school sex abuse cover-ups should be entitled to recover punitive, as well as compensatory, damages.

L.   Potential Negligent Infliction of Emotional Distress Claims

Under New York law, a plaintiff must adequately plead four elements to state a claim for negligent infliction of emotional distress: (1) breach of a duty owed to plaintiff, which breach either unreasonably endangered plaintiff's physical safety or caused plaintiff to fear for his physical safety; (2) extreme and outrageous conduct; (3) a causal connection between the conduct and the injury; and (4) severe emotional distress.[317]

---

[315] *Hutchins v. Utica Mutual Insur. Co.*, 107 A.D.2d 871, 873 (3d Dept. 1985) (in insured's action to recover compensatory and punitive damages against insurance carrier and its claim adjuster on basis of fraud and negligent misrepresentation arising from adjuster's advising them against consulting an attorney, question of fact as to whether defendants maliciously or recklessly discouraged plaintiffs from retaining counsel in order to promote a minimal settlement in favor of insurer precluded summary judgment on issue of punitive damages).

[316] *See* Chapter I.G, *supra.*

[317] *Bovsun v. Sanperi*, 61 N.Y.2d 219, 230-31 (1984).

For our purposes, a plaintiff may recover under a direct duty theory when "she suffers an emotional injury from defendant's breach of a duty which unreasonably endangered her own physical safety."[318]

The New York courts rarely permit negligent infliction of emotional distress claims to survive summary judgment, as they have narrowly construed the second element—extreme and outrageous conduct—of the tort.[319] New York law thus provides that a negligent infliction claim will not lie unless a defendant's conduct was "so outrageous in character, and so extreme in degree, as to go beyond all possible bounds of decency, and to be regarded as atrocious, and utterly intolerable in a civilized community."[320]

Romero v. City of New York is instructive. There, the Eastern District of New York Court held that the New York City Department of Education's ("NYCDOE") failure to report an incident of the sexual abuse of a student to law enforcement authorities did not constitute the requisite "outrageous conduct" to support a claim for negligent infliction of emotional distress.[321] In that case, though, the record established that the NYCDOE "took immediate, affirmative steps to commence an investigation by [a state agency] into a possibly inappropriate relationship between [the teacher and underage student] and to stop [the teacher's] sexual ... abuse of [the student] once the NYCDOE

---

[318] *Mortise v. U.S.*, 102 F.3d 693, 696 (2d Cir. 1996) (*citing, Kennedy v. McKesson Co.*, 58 N.Y.2d 500, 504 (1983)).

[319] *See e.g., Sheila C. v. Povich*, 11 A.D.3d 120, 130-31 (1st Dept. 2004) (dismissing claim); *Romero v. City of New York*, 839 F. Supp.2d 588, 620 & 631 (EDNY 2012) (same); *Naughright v. Weiss*, 826 F. Supp.2d 676, 697 (SDNY 2011)(same).

[320] *Naughright*, 826 F. Supp.2d at 697 (*quoting, Sheila C.*, 11 A.D.3d at 130-31).

[321] *Romero*, 839 F. Supp.2d at 629-31.

learned of it by immediately relieving [the teacher] of his teaching duties and removing him from [the school]."[322]

As school officials are held to an *in loco parentis* supervisory standard over children—and required by law to care for the children entrusted to them as if they were their own flesh and blood[323]—it is not difficult to fathom a cover-up scenario where a school's conduct is sufficiently "outrageous" to trigger a viable negligent infliction of emotional distress claim. A school sex abuse cover-up case could arguably meet the high "outrageous conduct" threshold if a plaintiff could plausibly allege that school officials permitted a known sexual predator to remain at the school and continue to sexually assault unsuspecting and largely defenseless children.[324]

Any particular school's conduct must be assessed on a case-by-case basis to ascertain whether its acts or omissions in support of a sex abuse cover-up were "beyond all possible bounds of decency," "atrocious," and "utterly intolerable in a civilized community."

In "old" school sex abuse cases, moreover, the negligence statute of limitations [CPLR § 214] mandates that a negligent infliction of emotional distress claim be filed within three years of plaintiff's injury. Accordingly, for a plaintiff to revive a *prima facie* untimely negligent infliction of emotional distress claim, he must trigger equitable estoppel. He must plead and prove, therefore, that he reasonably relied on defendants' *post-abuse* fraud,

---

[322] *Id.* at 629.

[323] *See* Chapter I.G, *supra.*

[324] Likewise, plaintiffs may argue that the school had a duty to protect them from foreseeable dangers, and breached that duty by permitting a known sexual predator to have easy access to children (including them). *See* Chapter II.A-D, *supra.*

misrepresentations, or deception which effectively prevented him from timely commencing the action.[325]

III.   VIABLE ACTIONS BASED UPON SCHOOL VIOLATIONS OF NEW YORK CONSUMER PROTECTION LAWS

A.   New York General Business Law § 349 Claims: Deceptive Acts or Practices

New York private schools are creatures of the marketplace. They compete in a highly competitive environment to induce parents to send their children to well-regarded elementary and secondary schools, at often substantial costs (for tuition, books, room and board, etc). These schools' direct involvement in commerce and constant solicitation of educational consumers make them subject to New York's consumer protection laws. New York General Business Law § 349, in certain circumstances, may thus be invoked by a plaintiff in "old" school sexual abuse cover-up cases.

The New York Consumer Protection Act codified at § 349 of The New York General Business Law ("GBL § 349") declares that "[d]eceptive acts or practices in the conduct of any business, trade, on commerce or in the furnishing of any service" in New York are unlawful."[326]

"To make out a *prima facie* case under Section 349, a plaintiff must demonstrate that (1) defendant's deceptive acts

---

[325] *See Philip F. v. Roman Catholic Diocese of Las Vegas*, 70 A.D.3d 765, 766 (2d Dept. 2010) (holding that diocese and priest were not equitably estopped from raising statutes of limitation defense). *See also*, Chapter I, *supra*.

[326] NY GBL ("GBL") § 349 (a).

were directed at consumers; (2) the acts are misleading in a material way; and (3) the plaintiff has been injured as a result."[327]

On its face, GBL § 349 applies "to virtually all economic activity, and its application has been correspondingly broad."[328] This consumer protection statute thus provides courts with the authority to "cope with the numerous, ever-changing types of false and deceptive business practices which plague consumers in our State."[329]

As currently understood, GBL § 349 "encompasses a significantly wider range of deceptive business practices that were never previously condemned by decisional law."[330] The gravamen of GBL § 349 is an act or practice that is "deceptive or misleading in a material way."[331] As such, "intent to defraud and justifiable reliance are not elements of the [GBL § 349] statutory claim."

New York courts have adopted an objective definition of "deceptive acts and practices," limiting that term to those acts or practices that are "likely to mislead a reasonable consumer acting reasonably under the circumstances."[332] Moreover, "[o]mission based claims under [GBL § 349] are appropriate where the business alone possesses material information that is relevant to the consumer and fails to provide this information."[333]

---

[327] *Maurizio v. Goldsmith*, 230 F.3d 518, 521 (2d Cir. 2000) (per curiam) (*citing, Oswego Laborers' Local 214 Pension Fund v. Marine Midland Bank*, 85 N.Y.2d 20, 25 (1995)).

[328] *Wilner v. Allstate Insur. Co.*, 71 A.D.3d 155, 160 (2d Dept. 2010) (citations omitted).

[329] *Karlin v. IVF America, Inc.*, 93 N.Y.2d 282, 290-91 (1991).

[330] *Id.*; *see also, Gaidon*, 94 N.Y.2d at 343; *Wilner*, 71 A.D.3d at 160 (The statute, moreover, was intended to be "broadly applicable, extending far beyond the reach of common law fraud.").

[331] *Wilner*, 71 A.D.3d at 162; *Small v. Lorillard Tobacco Co.*, 94 N.Y.2d 43, 55 (1999); *Oswego*, 85 N.Y.2d at 25.

[332] *Oswego*, 85 N.Y.2d at 26; *see also, Karlin*, 93 N.Y.2d at 294.

[333] *Bildstein v. MasterCard Int'l, Inc.*, 2005 WL 1324972, *4 (SDNY 2005)

In the school-student context, the acts or practices of a school are "consumer-oriented" if they were "part and parcel of [a school's] efforts to sell its services as a ... school to prospective students."[334] GBL § 349 thus applies to educational contracts.[335]

Drew v. Sylvan Learning Center Corp.[336] is illuminative. There, a parent who had enrolled her child in a tutoring program offered by defendant, a tutoring business, asserted, *inter alia*, a claim for deceptive business practices in violation of GBL § 349.[337]

Plaintiff claimed that the actionable "deceptive act" of defendant was the program's guarantee that children would improve at least one grade level equivalent in reading or math within thirty-six hours of instruction. She claimed that the guarantee, which was contained in the program's brochures, deceived her into enrolling her child into the school's program.[338]

The Court concluded that defendant deceived consumers, including plaintiff, and violated GBL § 349, by guaranteeing that its services would improve her children's grade levels and implying that its standards were aligned with those of the Board of Education.[339] The deception led plaintiff to believe that defendant's services would improve her children's grade levels and induced her to "incur[ ] the expense of paying for the

---

(*quoting, Oswego*, 85 N.Y.2d at 26).

[334] *Gomez-Jiminez v. New York Law School*, 2012 WL 662062, *2 (1st Dept. 2012) (*citing, Chais v. Technical Career Insts.*, 2002 WL 34433891, *11-12 (Sup. Ct. NY Cty. 2002)).

[335] *See Cambridge v. Telemarketing Concepts, Inc.*, 171 Misc. 2d 796, 802 (City Ct., City of Yonkers 1997); *Brown v. Hambric*, 168 Misc. 2d 502, 506-07 (City Ct., City of Yonkers 1995); *Andre v. Pace Univ.*, 170 Misc. 2d 893, 896 (App. Term, 2d Dept. 1996).

[336] 16 Misc. 3d 836 (Civil Ct., City of Yonkers 2007).

[337] *Id.* at 837-38.

[338] *Id.* at 839-40.

[339] *Id.* at 841.

defendant's program."[340]

The use of GBL § 349 in a school cover-up of sex abuse case is a creative but appropriate application of the statute.[341] Such claims should allege that the school engaged in actionable "deceptive acts and practices" when it induced plaintiffs to enroll in (or stay at) the school though materially false representations (indeed, a materially false central premise): that the school was safe and its faculty members, including the known sexually abusive teacher or coach, were trustworthy. For plaintiffs to plead viable Section 349 claims, moreover, they do not have to plead justifiable reliance on the subject misrepresentations.[342]

Plaintiffs asserting GBL § 349 claims against schools for "deceptive acts and practices" which led to sexual abuse injuries, should take care to emphasize in their pleadings that these claims do not sound in "educational malpractice." Plaintiffs should not ask a court to "make judgments as to the validity of broad educational policies."[343]

Plaintiffs in a school sex abuse cover-up case should thus not argue that the schools failed to provide them with an "effective education." Rather, they should claim that the school failed to provide them with a safe school environment, and failed to keep them safe from a known sexual predator, through deception, and that these acts (of commission and omission) and practices led directly to their injuries.

Plaintiffs alleging these kind of GBL § 349 claims should allege "actual damages" resulting from their sexual abuse, such as

---

[340] *Id.*

[341] *See Wilner*, 71 A.D.3d at 160.

[342] *See id.* at 162; *Small*, 94 N.Y.2d at 55.

[343] *Andre*, 170 Misc. 2d at 876; *see also, Paladino v. Adelphi Univ.*, 89 A.D.2d 85, 89-90 (a claim is not cognizable (i.e., it is a barred "educational malpractice" claim) if "the essence of the complaint is that the school breached its agreement by failing to provide an effective education").

psychological counseling expenses, and perhaps even a partial refund of the tuition paid to the school under false pretenses.[344] The latter element of damages, tuition refunds, must be pled carefully to avoid the charge that plaintiffs' GBL § 349 claims actually sound in non-actionable "educational malpractice."[345]

B.   New York General Business Law § 350 Claims: False Advertising

Similarly, a cause of action for false advertising pursuant to General Business Law § 350 may be stated so long as plaintiffs allege that "the advertisement (1) had an impact on consumers at large; (2) was deceptive or misleading in a material way; and (3) resulted in injury."[346]

"The standard for recovery under General Business Law § 350, while specific to false advertising, is otherwise identical to Section 349."[347]

---

[344] *See People v. McNair*, 2005 WL 2780976, *1 (Sup. Ct. NY Cty. 2005) (Defendant violated GBL §§ 349 & 350 by making numerous misrepresentations about a private school in Harlem which closed abruptly and without notice; parents of children enrolled at school were entitled to all fees paid to the school); *Dungan v. The Academy at Ivy Ridge*, 249 F.R.D. 413, 419 (NDNY 2008) (school for troubled teens violated GBL § § 349 & 350 by falsely stating in its promotional materials that its graduates would earn high school diplomas and that it was accredited by Northwest Association of Schools and Colleges; school and New York State Attorney General agreed that, *inter alia*, school would make partial tuition refunds to each student who received diploma).

[345] *See* note 160, *supra*. Plaintiffs who succeed in their GBL § 349 claims are also entitled to recover reasonable attorneys' fees incurred in the prosecution of the action. NY General Business Law § 349(h).

[346] *Andre Strishak & Assoc. v. Hewlett Packard Co.*, 300 A.D.2d 608, 609 (3d Dept. 2002).

[347] *Denenberg v. Rosen*, 71 A.D.3d 187, 194 (1st Dept. 2010), *lv. dismissed,*

It is axiomatic in New York that the rights and obligations of the parties, as contained in a school's bulletins and catalogs, become a part of a contract between a school and a student.[348] A former student who can allege that he relied on false representations contained in a school's recruitment or advertising brochures, or catalogs or handbooks, as to the safety of a school or trustworthiness of a teacher or coach, can thus possibly allege a GBL § 350 claim against the school if such false advertisements induced him to enroll in (or stay at) the school— and he was subsequently sexually assaulted by a known sexual predator.[349] Plaintiff must, however, plead the false advertising statement(s) with some specificity; he cannot rely merely on general statements.[350]

---

14 N.Y.3d 910 (2010).

[348] *See Vought v. Teachers College, Columbia Univ.*, 127 A.D.2d 654, 655 (2d Dept. 1987); *Prusack v. State of New York*, 117 A.D.2d 729, 730 (2d Dept. 1986); *Andre*, 170 Misc. 2d at 876.

[349] Unlike in a § 349 claim, reliance on the false advertising statement is a *prima facie* element of a § 350 claim. *Williams v. The Dow Chemical Co.*, 2004 WL 1348932, 21 (SDNY 2004) (but, "in the fraud context, New York state courts have held that parental reliance on false or misleading statements by an advertiser may be imputed to a child.") (*citing, Ruffing v. Union Carbide Corp.*, 308 A.D.2d 526, 528 (2d Dept. 2003)).

[350] *See Linsky v. NYNEX Corp.*, 1997 WL 1048597, *2 (Sup. Ct. NY Cty. 1997).

C.   Statute of Limitations Issues for General Business Law Claims

The New York Court of Appeals has recently affirmed that General Business Law § 349 claims are "subject to the three-year limitations period imposed by CPLR § 214(2), which applies to actions 'to recover upon a liability ... created or imposed by statute.'"[351]

A *prima facie* untimely GBL § 349 claim, however, may still be viable, pursuant to equitable estoppel, if a plaintiff can establish that defendants made fraudulent misrepresentations and/or took affirmative measures to conceal their wrongdoing within the limitations period (i.e., within three years from when the GBL § 349 claim began to run).[352] Equitable tolling of GBL § 349 claims "is [thus] available in cases of fraudulent concealment."[353]

In a school sex abuse cover-up case, plaintiffs should thus plead the same facts needed to equitably toll their *prima facie* untimely negligent retention and supervision claims in order to equitably toll their GBL § 349 claims.

Plaintiffs should also note that although pre-abuse reliance is not an element of a GBL § 349 claim, they will need to plead and prove that they justifiably relied on defendants' post-

---

[351] *Corsello v. Verizon New York, Inc.*, 18 N.Y.3d 777, 789 (2012) (*citing, Gaidon v. Guardian Life Insur. Co. of Am.*, 96 N.Y.2d 201, 208 (2001)).

[352] *See Council v. Better Homes Depot, Inc.*, 2006 WL 2376381, *11 (EDNY 2006) (Plaintiff's GBL § 349 claim equitably tolled where defendants allegedly made "fraudulent misrepresentations of material fact and fraudulent concealment of material facts" to induce plaintiffs to proceed with transaction).

[353] *M&T Mortgage Corp. v. Miller*, 323 F. Supp.2d 405, 411 (EDNY 2004); *see also Gaidon*, 96 N.Y.2d at 210 (GBL § 349 claim accrues when the plaintiff "has been injured by a deceptive act or practice.").

abuse misrepresentations, fraud, or deception, in order to equitably toll these claims.[354]

IV. TITLE IX CLAIMS MAY BE A VIABLE LAST RESORT FOR A PLAINTIFF LONG AGO ABUSED BY A TEACHER IN SCHOOL

If a plaintiff's negligence and/or General Business Law §§ 349 and 350 claims are time-barred, and she can not plead any pre-abuse fraud (giving rise to an independent fraud claim) or any post-abuse fraud, misrepresentations, or deceptions (tolling or stopping the running of the statute of limitations on her non-fraud claims), then a Title IX claim against the school may be her *only* remedy against a culpable school. The potential delayed accrual of that claim, pursuant to the federal discovery rule, thus deserves close scrutiny.

A viable Title IX claim also raises a federal question and thus allows a plaintiff to obtain federal jurisdiction and file suit in federal court, which may—depending on the circumstances—have significant strategic value.[355]

---

[354] *See Zimmerman*, 888 F. Supp.2d at 341. *See also*, Chapter I.E, *supra*.
[355] A prevailing plaintiff in a Title IX case is also entitled to recover her reasonable attorneys' fees. *See* The Civil Rights Attorneys' Fees Award Act of 1976, Pub. L. 94-559, 90 Stat. 2641, as set forth in 42 U.S.C. § 1988.

A. Basic Title IX Principles in the Sexual Abuse Context

Title IX of the Education Amendments of 1972[356] provides in pertinent part that:

> No person in the United States shall, on the basis of sex, be excluded from participation in, be denied the benefits of, or be subjected to discrimination under any education program or activity receiving Federal financial assistance.

Under Title IX, a school will incur liability if it is: (1) deliberately indifferent; (2) to known acts of discrimination; (3) which occur under its control.[357] Specifically, the school's "deliberate indifference must either directly cause the abuse to occur or make students vulnerable to such abuse, and that abuse must take place in a context subject to the [school's] control."[358]

Title IX provides a private cause of action against a recipient of federal funds for discrimination based on sex,[359] and sexual harassment and sexual abuse clearly constitute discrimination under Title IX.[360] A single sexual assault constitutes severe and objectively offensive sexual harassment for Title IX purposes.[361]

---

[356] Pub. L. No. 92-318, 86 Stat. 235, 373 (1972) (codified as amended at 20 U.S.C. §§ 1681-1688 (1994)).

[357] *Davis v. Monroe County Bd. of Educ.*, 526 U.S. 629, 642 (1999).

[358] *Id.* at 645.

[359] *Cannon v. Univ. of Chicago*, 441 U.S. 677, 708-09 (1979).

[360] *Franklin v. Gwinnett County Public Schools*, 503 U.S. 60, 75 (1992).

[361] *Bliss v. Putnam Valley Central School District*, 2011 WL 1079944, *5 (SDNY 2011).

In a school sex abuse cover-up case, a Title IX plaintiff must show that an official of the school who had authority to institute corrective measures on the school's behalf had actual (not just merely constructive) notice of, and was deliberately indifferent to, the teacher's misconduct.[362] Title IX's actual notice standard is satisfied "by knowledge of a 'substantial risk of serious harm' in a context where ... multiple prior allegations of sexual abuse were lodged against a teacher ..., so that his proclivities for such abuse were well known."[363]

Although most Title IX cases involve public schools, "Title IX [also] regulates private schools who choose to receive federal funding."[364] The threshold inquiry in any Title IX case, which at times becomes complicated, is whether a school is a recipient of federal financial assistance and thus subject to the provisions of Title IX.

B.   A School that Receives "Federal Financial Assistance" (in Various Forms) is Subject to Title IX

The Department of Justice Regulations, 28 C.F.R. § 54.105 (2012), define "federal financial assistance" for the purpose of Title IX to include: (1) federal financial aid paid to a school's students; and (2) federal loans made to a school for construction and/or rehabilitation projects. If a school's students receive federal financial aid and/or the school received federal

---

[362] *See Tesoriero v. Syosset Central School District*, 382 F. Supp.2d 387, 396 (EDNY 2005).

[363] *Zamora v. North Salem Central School District*, 414 F. Supp.2d 418, 424 (SDNY 2006).

[364] *Litman v. George Mason Univ.*, 5 F. Supp.2d 366, 373 (E.D. Va. 1998) (Only schools can be held liable under Title IX); *Folkes v. N.Y. Coll. of Osteopathic Med.*, 214 F. Supp.2d 273, 282 (EDNY 2002) ("Individuals, [such as school employees or representatives,] cannot be held liable.").

construction loans during the time plaintiffs suffered discrimination (based on their sex abuse), then the school is a federal funding "recipient" and subject to Title IX.

Likewise, at least one circuit court has held that a private school's tax-exempt status might constitute "federal financial assistance" so as to make it subject to Title IX.[365] In *Zimmerman*, though, Judge Block rejected plaintiffs' argument that Poly Prep's tax-exempt status, by itself, made Poly Prep a recipient of federal funds.[366]

The extensive entanglement of the federal government into education at a state-wide level for the last half century has exponentially increased the number of private and parochial schools which receive federal funds and are therefore potentially subject to Title IX. Schools which receive federal funds pursuant to federal programs such as the National School Lunch Program,[367] and federal grants for library inventories and/or audio-visual equipment,[368] thus become vulnerable to Title IX

---

[365] See *M.H.D. v. Westminster Schools*, 172 F.3d 797, 801-02 (11th Cir. 1999) (plaintiff's argument—that an exemption from federal taxes produced the same result as a direct federal grant, the school possessed funds that otherwise would belong to the Government—was "neither immaterial or wholly frivolous."). *See also, McGlotten v. Connally*, 338 F. Supp. 448, 461 (D.D.C. 1972) (a tax exemption constituted "federal financial assistance" in the context of Title VI; as *M.H.D.* noted, because Title IX was modeled after Title VI); *Fulani v. League of Women Voters Educ. Fund*, 684 F. Supp. 1185, 1192 (SDNY 1988) (court concluded that defendant received "federal financial assistance" within the meaning of both Title VI *and Title IX* because it received both direct grants and tax-exempt status) (emphasis in original)).

[366] 888 F. Supp.2d at 332 n.2.

[367] See *Valesky v. Aquinas Academy*, 2011 WL 4102584, *10 (W.D. Pa. 2011); *Russo v. Diocese of Greensburg*, 2010 WL 3656579,* 4 (W.D. Pa. 2010).

[368] The enactment of The Elementary and Secondary Education Act of 1965

claims.

Under some circumstances, moreover, a school which does not receive any federal funds may still be liable under Title IX based on an affiliated entity's receipt of such funds.

C.   A School May Be Deemed a "Recipient" of Federal Funds (Thus Subjecting It to Title IX) Even When It Does Not Directly Receive Federal Funds, If a Closely Affiliated School or "School System" Receives Federal Financial Assistance

The Civil Rights Restoration Act of 1987, codified as amended at 20 U.S.C. § 1687 (2002), as discussed below (in Chapter IV.D, *infra*), broadened the definition of "program or activity" under Title IX. Section 1687 provides, in the context of non-public educational institutions, that the term "program or activity" (and "program") means all the operations of "a[n] other school system."[369] "In other words, if any part of a covered school

---

("ESEA")(P.L. 89-10), on April 9, 1965, "revolutionized the federal government's role in education." Brian K. Landsberg "Elementary and Secondary Education Act of 1965," *Major Acts of Congress Vol. 1.*, http://www.enotes.com/topics/elementary-secondary-education-act-1965#reference-elementary-secondary-education-act-1965, "Congress has reauthorized the ESEA several times since its initial passage, most recently in 2002 [as 'The No Child Left Behind Act']." *Id.* Pursuant to this law, the federal government provides funding to approximately 90 percent of the nation's public and parochial schools. Monies are provided to schools, *inter alia*, to meet the needs of "educationally deprived" children, purchase library materials and audio/visual equipment, and fund school radio and television, counseling, and foreign language programs." *Id.* If a sexual abuse survivor can plausibly allege that his school received ESEA funds in more than a *de minimus* amount, he may establish that his school is a "recipient" of federal funds and thus subject to potential Title IX liability.
[369] 20 U.S.C. § 1687 (2)(B); 29 U.S.C. § 794 (b)(2)(b).

system [or school] receives federal financial assistance, then all the operations of that school system [or school] are subject to the provisions of Title IX."[370]

Consistent with this approach, federal regulations define a "recipient" of federal financial assistance as

> Any public or private agency, institution or organization, or other entity, or any person, to whom federal financial assistance is extended directly or through another recipient and which operates an educational program or activity which receives or benefits from such assistance, including any subunit, successor, assignee, or transferee thereof.[371]

"Thus, an entity may receive federal financial assistance indirectly and still be considered a recipient for purposes of Title IX."[372]

In *Russo v. Diocese of Greensberg*, the school that allegedly violated Title IX did not receive federal funds. Yet another high school in the same diocese, as well as several elementary schools, participated in the National School Lunch Program.[373] The court imputed the recipient school's receipt of federal financial assistance to the diocese and all schools located within the

---

[370] *Valesky v. Aquinas Academy*, 2011 WL 4102584, *10 (W.D. Pa. 2011) (*citing, Nat'l Collegiate Athletic Ass'n v. Smith*, 525 U.S. 459, 465-66 (1999); *Russo v. Diocese of Greensburg*, 2010 WL 3656579, *4 (W.D. Pa. 2010) ("prohibition of discrimination applied to the entire institution and all of its operations, programs and activities whenever it received any federal funds at all")).

[371] 34 C.F.R. § 106.2 (h).

[372] *Valesky*, 2011 WL 4102584 at *10 (*citing, Smith v. Nat'l Collegiate Athletic Ass'n*, 266 F.3d 152, 160 (3d Cir. 2001).

[373] *Russo*, 2010 WL 3656579 at *6.

diocese (including the defendant school).[374]

The mere fact, that one school may have independent legal status from another is thus not necessarily dispositive.[375]

A court, in analyzing the threshold issue of whether a school which does not directly receive federal funds (but which is affiliated with a diocese or other potential "school system" which receives federal funds) should be considered a recipient of federal funds for Title IX purposes, should consider: (1) whether the school is closely managed by the diocese or other potential school system; (2) who appoints (and employs) the top administrators at the school; (3) which entity can authorize the school to close; (4) whether the diocese or potential school system provides a handbook or written guidelines for the students at the school; (5) which entity provides financial support to the school; (6) whether the diocese or potential school system provides the school with further support in the form of payroll services, an intranet, telecommunications, and information technologies equipment; (7) whether any staff is shared; and (8) whether there is any written institutional affiliation agreements between the school and other entities.[376]

---

[374] See id. (defendants consistently represented that the recipient school had no legal status separate from the diocese).

[375] Valesky, 2011 WL 4102584 at *10; see also, Homer v. Kentucky High School Athletic Ass'n, 43 F.3d 265, 272 (6th Cir. 1994), cert. denied, 531 U.S. 824 (2000) ("Congress has made clear its intent to extend the scope of Title IX's ... obligations to the furthest reaches of an institution's programs. We will not defeat that purpose by recognizing artificial distinctions in the structure or operation of an institution.").

[376] See Valesky, 2011 WL 4102584 at *11 (holding that if the diocese receives federal financial assistance then, given the extensive entanglement of the diocese into the schools' financial and administrative affairs, all the schools within the diocese—even those which do not receive federal financial assistance—are subject to the provisions of Title IX); see also, Buckley v. Archdiocese of Rockville Ctr., 992 F. Supp. 586 (EDNY 1998)

There is no bright-line rule as to when a school's affiliation with a diocese, or other school system, is sufficient to impute the federal financial assistance received by the latter to the former. A court should reduce this issue to one simple question: *does the diocese, or other potential school system, have extensive involvement, administratively, financially, or both, in the non-recipient school?* If the answer, balancing all relevant factors, is affirmative, then the non-recipient school should be subject to Title IX.[377]

If a school contends that it is not a recipient of federal financial assistance, and thus not subject to Title IX, plaintiffs who make non-frivolous assertions that the school receives categories of funding "within the meaning of Title IX" should be entitled to reasonable discovery on that threshold question.[378]

(Diocese and Catholic School which did not receive federal funds could not be liable under Title IX based on receipt of federal assistance by public school district, where there were no formal agreements or fund-sharing).

[377] See *Valesky*, 2011 WL 4102584 at *11.

[378] See *Henschke v. New York Hospital-Cornell Medical Center*, 821 F. Supp. 166, 172 (SDNY 1993)(court converted defendants' (teaching hospital and medical school) motion to dismiss into a motion for summary judgment, and permitted plaintiffs to obtain discovery on whether defendants were recipients of federal funds within ambit of Title IX); *see also, Communities for Equity v. Michigan High School Athletic Ass'n*, 26 F. Supp.2d 1001, 1009 (W.D. Mich. 1998)(Court granted plaintiffs' Fed. R. Civ. Pro. 56 (f) motion to conduct discovery before having to respond to defendants' summary judgment motion; plaintiffs were entitled to adequate opportunity "to inquire into the facts" supporting their Title IX claim).

D. **"Discrimination" in Any School Program or Activity Subjects the Entire School to Title IX: The Restoration Act of 1987 Applies Retroactively**

In its 1984 decision, *Grove City College v. Bell*,[379] the Supreme Court held that the term "education program or activity" in Title IX required a plaintiff asserting a claim thereunder to allege that the discrimination occurred within a particular program or activity within the school, and that the federal funds were directed to such program or activity, not the school as a whole. This decision was promptly overturned by Congress with the enactment of the Restoration Act of 1987 (the "Restoration Act"),[380] which provided in pertinent part:

> For the purposes of this title, the term "program or activity" and "program" mean all of ... the operations of an entire corporation, partnership, or other private organization, or an entire sole proprietorship if assistance is extended to such corporation, partnership, private organization, or sole proprietorship as a whole; or which is principally engaged in the business of providing education, health care, housing, social services, or parks and recreation...

Courts in the Second Circuit have expressly held that the Restoration Act's instruction regarding the original intent of Title IX applies retroactively.[381]

In *Leake v. Long Island Jewish Medical Center*, indeed, the Court held that the Restoration Act should be applied

---

[379] 465 U.S. 555, 573-74 (1984).

[380] Pub. L. No. 100-259, 102 Stat. 28 (1988), codified as amended at 20 U.S.C. § 1687.

[381] *See Zimmerman*, 888 F. Supp.2d at 332-33 (citations omitted).

retroactively.[382]   Specifically, the Court held that although the Restoration Act does not include a provision stating that it should be applied retroactively, "the use of the terms "restore" and "clarify" indicate that Congress did not intend to change the statute; rather it intended to reject the Supreme Court's interpretation."[383] The Court thus emphasized that "the Second Circuit has found that ... Congress intended to 'codify a congressional purpose long in place which Congress believes the Supreme Court has misinterpreted.'"[384]

The *Leake* Court concluded that the stated purpose of the Restoration Act "is not to amend but to "restore" and "clarify.""[385] The amendment at issue was "directed at overruling a Supreme Court interpretation of a statute" and, as such, the Court was "compelled to apply the Restoration Act retroactively."[386] The legislative history of the Restoration Act supported *Leake's* conclusion.[387]

As Judge Block pointed out in *Zimmerman*,[388] in reexamining this issue, although *Leake* has not been overruled,

---

[382] 695 F. Supp. 1414, 1417 (EDNY 1988), *aff'd*, 869 F.2d 130 (2d Cir. 1989). The *Leake* case arose out of § 504 of the Rehabilitation Act (29 U.S.C. § 794) which contains similar statutory language to Title IX and which is likewise subject to the Restoration Act of 1987.

[383] *Id.* at 1417.

[384] *Id.* (*citing, Mrs. W. v. Tirozzi*, 832 F.2d 748, 755 (2d Cir. 1987) (Second Circuit inferred Congressional intent for retroactive application of amendment to Education of the Handicapped Act, 20 U.S.C. §§ 1400-85 (West 1978 and Supp. 1988) because legislative history included an expressed Congressional intent to "reestablish rights" and "reaffirm ... the viability" [of the prior statute].).

[385] *Id.*

[386] *Id.*

[387] *Id.*

[388] 888 F. Supp.2d at 332.

the Supreme Court's decision in *Landgraf v. USI Film Products*,[389] adds clarity to the analysis. In *Landgraf*, the Supreme Court stated:

> When a case implicates a federal statute enacted after the events in suit, the court's first task is to determine whether Congress has expressly prescribed the statute's proper reach. When . . . the statute contains no such express command, the court must determine whether the new statute would have retroactive effect, i.e., whether it would impair rights a party possessed when he acted, increase a party's liability for past conduct, or impose new duties with respect to transactions already completed. If the statute would operate retroactively, our traditional presumption teaches that it does not govern absent clear congressional intent favoring such a result.[390]

In *Zimmerman*, the Court did not determine whether *Landgraf* required it to disregard *Leake's* holding. That issue was rendered moot because *Leake's* "discussion of the [Restoration] Act's wording and legislative history remains instructive," and thus compelled the Court to conclude that "those factors demonstrate the necessary 'clear congressional intent' favoring retroactive application [of the Restoration Act]."[391]

The Restoration Act did not "in any way alter [ ] the existing rights of action and the corresponding remedies permissible under Title IX."[392] Rather, Congress sought merely "to correct what it considered to be an unacceptable decision" by

---

[389] 511 U.S. 244, 280 (1994).

[390] *Id.* at 280.

[391] *Zimmerman*, 888 F. Supp.2d at 333.

[392] *Franklin v. Gwinnett County Public Schools*, 503 U.S. 60, 73 (1992).

the Supreme Court in *Grove City*.[393]

Simply stated, the Restoration Act did not change Title IX. Rather, it merely codified the original purpose of Title IX which was misinterpreted by the Supreme Court in *Grove City*.[394]

The Restoration Act should thus be applied retroactively to all Title IX claims governing conduct which occurred any time after Title IX's enactment on June 23, 1972. As such, if any designated "recipient" school discriminates on the basis of gender (through sex abuse) in any of its programs or activities, then the entire school is subject to the provisions of Title IX.

E.   The Federal Discovery Rule Should Delay Accrual of a Plaintiff's Title IX Sexual Discrimination (Based on Sexual Abuse) Claim Until Plaintiff Discovers or Should Have Discovered the School's, Rather than the Abuser's, Misconduct

When a plaintiff asserts a Title IX claim for gender discrimination based upon sexual assault, his claim is subject to a three-year statute of limitations borrowed from the state law statute of limitations [CPLR § 214(5)] for personal injuries.[395] The borrowing of a state-law statute of limitations carries with it the borrowing of the state's "coordinate tolling rules."[396]

The pivotal point, often overlooked, is that the accrual of a federal claim—in other words, the determination of when a statute of limitations begins to run— "is a question of federal law that is not resolved by reference to state law."[397]

---

[393] *Id.*

[394] *See Leake*, 695 F. Supp. at 1417; *Mrs. W.*, 832 F.2d at 755; *Zimmerman*, 888 F. Supp.2d at 332-33.

[395] *See Curto v. Edmundson*, 392 F.3d 502, 504 (2d Cir. 2004).

[396] *Board of Regents v. Tomanio*, 446 U.S. 478, 484 (1980).

[397] *Wallace v. Kato*, 549 U.S. 384, 388 (2007); *see also, Zimmerman*, 888 F.

A Title IX claim brought by a plaintiff alleging gender discrimination based on sexual assault cannot rely upon any distinct statute of limitation as set forth in that statute. Title IX is silent on that point. A Title IX claim brought in New York must therefore borrow New York State's three year statute of limitations for personal injury actions [CPLR § 214(5)]; but, the pivotal issue of when that statute began to run—its accrual date— is governed by federal law. In the context of a school sex abuse cover-up case, this is a distinction with a difference.

As a threshold matter, it is well-settled in the Second Court (and other federal courts) that because the statute of limitations is an affirmative defense, the burden is on the defendant to establish when a federal claim accrues[398] When the federal discovery rule applies to a defendant's statute of limitations defense, the defendant has the burden of proving that plaintiff discovered, or in the exercise of reasonable diligence should have discovered, his claim against defendant prior to the statute of limitations cut-off.[399]

According to the Supreme Court, moreover, even if a plaintiff were placed on "inquiry notice" against a defendant based on his "suspicious" conduct, "the discovery rule would trigger the limitations period at that point, only if a reasonable person in her position would have learned of the inquiry in the exercise of due diligence."[400]

Supp.2d at 333.

[398] *Overall v. Estate of Klotz*, 52 F.2d 398, 403 (2d Cir. 1995) (defendant must make *prima facie* showing); *Gonzales v. Hasty*, 651 F.3d 318, 322 (2d Cir. 2011) (*citing*, Fed. R. Civ. Pro. 89(c)); *Atlantic Int'l Movers v. Ocean World Lines*, 914 F.Supp. 2d 267, 279 (EDNY 2012).

[399] *See Owner-Operator Independent v. Comerica Bank*, 860 F. Supp.2d 519, 544 (S.D. Ohio 2012)

[400] *TRW Inc.*, 534 U.S. 19, 30 (2001); *see also*, *Merck*, 130 S. Ct at 1796-99 (Supreme Court, in a detailed accrual analysis, held that defendant had

A court should thus place the burden of proof on a school defendant to establish that a sex abuse plaintiff could have earlier discovered facts demonstrating school officials' deliberate indifference in the face of their actual knowledge that a school employee had a propensity to assault children. This appropriate burden shift prevents a court from making plaintiffs prove a negative—a Herculean if not almost impossible task—and should go a long way towards holding truly culpable schools liable for Title IX damages.

The next issue, then, becomes when a school defendant can establish—with *prima* facie proof—a Title IX sex abuse case accrued. Judge Block, in *Zimmerman*, set forth the appropriate federal accrual standard:

> As a matter of federal law, "a claim generally accrues once the plaintiff knows or has reason to know of the injury which is the basis of the action." The knowledge required is minimal; the plaintiff need only have "knowledge of the injury's existence and knowledge of its cause or the person or entity that inflicted it."[401]

In *Zimmerman*, plaintiffs, citing *Keating v. Carey*,[402] argued that "when the defendant fraudulently conceals the wrong, the time does not begin running until the plaintiff discovers, or by the exercise of reasonable diligence should have discovered, the cause of action." Plaintiffs thus contended that, as a matter of federal law, *Keating* establishes that fraudulent concealment postpones accrual.[403]

---

the burden of showing when a reasonably diligent plaintiff would have discovered the facts constituting the alleged securities fraud violation).

[401] *Id.* (internal citations omitted).

[402] 706 F.2d 377, 382 (2d Cir. 1983).

[403] *Zimmerman*, 888 F. Supp.2d at 333.

Judge Block noted that a subsequent Second Circuit decision, *Pearl v. City of Long Beach*,[404] called *Keating's* rule on delayed accrual into question.[405] The *Pearl* Court noted that the language used in *Keating*—"the time does not begin running"— did not square with the result, which was to borrow New York's doctrine of equitable estoppel.[406] The Second Circuit, in *Pearl*, left the issue unresolved because in both *Keating* and *Pearl* "the conceptual difference between an accrual rule and a tolling rule was academic."[407]

Judge Block, in the absence of clear guidance from the Second Circuit, then turned to Judge Posner's oft-cited decision in *Cada v. Baxter Healthcare Corp.*,[408] to support his finding that fraudulent concealment is a "tolling doctrine"—and that the Court must borrow New York law regarding fraudulent concealment in a tolling context.[409]

> Fraudulent concealment in the law of limitations presupposes, that the plaintiff has discovered, or, as required by the discovery rule, should have discovered that the defendant injured him, and denotes efforts by the defendant—above and beyond the wrongdoing upon which the plaintiff's claim is founded—to prevent the plaintiff from suing in time.[410]

---

[404] 296 F.3d 76, 83 (2d Cir. 2002).

[405] *Zimmerman*, 888 F. Supp.2d at 333.

[406] *Id.* (*citing, Pearl*, 296 F.3d at 83 n.6).

[407] *Id.* (citing, *Pearl*, 296 F.3d at 84 ["the plaintiff's] current claims are barred whether the issue is viewed as one of delayed accrual or tolling.")).

[408] 920 F.2d 446 (7th Cir. 1990).

[409] Judge Block also noted that the Second Circuit, in *Veltri v. Building Serv. 32B-J Pension Fund*, 393 F.3d 318, 323 (2d Cir. 2004), cited *Cada* with approval. *Id.* at 333.

[410] *Zimmerman*, 888 F. Supp.2d at 334 (*quoting, Cada*, 920 F.2d at 451).

In *Cada*, an age discrimination in employment case, Judge Posner examined the differences between the accrual of the plaintiff's claim and the tolling of the statute of limitations.[411] "Accrual is the date on which the statute of limitations begins to run. It is not the date on which the wrong that injures the plaintiff occurs, but the date—often the same, but sometimes later —on which the plaintiff discovers that he has been injured."[412] Tolling doctrines, on the other hand, "stop the statute of limitations from running even if the accrual date has passed."[413]

Judge Posner emphasized that "the rule that postpones the beginning of the limitations period from the date when the plaintiff is wronged to the date when he discovers he has been injured, is the "discovery rule" of federal common law, which is read into statutes of limitations in federal–question cases (even when those statutes of limitations are borrowed from state law) in the absence of a contrary directive from Congress."[414]

Cada thus held that although equitable estoppel in the limitations setting is sometimes called fraudulent concealment, the analysis changes where the defendant in a fraud case makes an effort to conceal the fraud. "To the extent that such efforts [to conceal a fraud] succeed, they postpone the date of accrual by preventing the plaintiff from discovering that he is a victim of fraud."[415] A defendant's success in preventing a plaintiff from

---

[411] 920 F.2d at 450-51.

[412] *Id.* at 450.

[413] *Id.*

[414] *Id.* (*citing, inter alia, Cullen v. Margrotta*, 811 F.2d 698, 725 (2d Cir. 1987)). In an age discrimination suit against a school based on denial of tenure, therefore, the statute of limitations does not begin to accrue until the time the discriminatory act, the tenure decision, was made by the school and communicated to the employee at issue. *Id.* (*citing, Delaware State College v. Ricks*, 449 U.S. 250, 258 (1980)).

[415] *Id.* (citation omitted).

discovering that he has been the victim of a fraud, "thus [falls] within the domain of the discovery rule" and delays the accrual of a federal claim.[416]

On the other hand, "fraudulent concealment in the law of limitations presupposes that the plaintiff has discovered, or, as required by the discovery rule, should have discovered, *that the defendant injured him ...*"[417] Fraudulent concealment, as a basis for equitable estoppel, thus "denotes efforts by the defendant [independent] of the wrongdoing upon which the plaintiff's claim is founded ... to prevent the plaintiff from suing in time.[418] Judge Posner noted that equitable estoppel would be triggered, for instance, if defendant had told plaintiff that it would not plead the statute of limitations as a defense to any suit for age discrimination he might bring, or if defendant forged documents purporting to negate any basis for supporting that plaintiff's termination was related to his age.[419]

Judge Posner's scholarly and tightly reasoned decision in *Cada* suggests that the federal discovery rule, which delays accrual of a borrowed state statute of limitations, may, in appropriate circumstances, be invoked in a Title IX claim based on a teacher's sexual abuse of a student. The threshold inquiry as to whether the federal discovery rule is applicable is *did the plaintiff know or have reason to know of the injury which is the basis of his action.*[420]

In *Zimmerman* the Court correctly noted that in a tolling context, the federal court was required to borrow New York law on fraudulent concealment.[421] But the *Zimmerman* Court by-

---

[416] *Id.*

[417] *Id.* (emphasis added).

[418] *Id.*

[419] *Id.* at 451.

[420] *See Cornwell v. Robinson,* 23 F.3d 694, 703 (2d Cir. 1994); *Zimmerman,* 888 F. Supp.2d at 333.

[421] 888 F. Supp.2d at 333.

passed a detailed analysis as to whether the plaintiffs had discovered, or should have discovered, that the Poly Prep defendant injured them.[422] The *Zimmerman* Court implicitly suggested, or at least appeared to assume, that the injuries that triggered the running of the borrowed state statute of limitations for plaintiffs' Title IX claims were the actual sexual abuse acts committed by the school's football coach. But, especially because a Title IX claim may be maintained only against a school, rather than individuals employed by a school,[423] the *Zimmerman* Court's assumption as to this threshold issue was incorrect. As *Cada* illustrates, the borrowed statute of limitations only begins to run on the date the plaintiff discovers, or should have discovered, that the school itself injured him.[424]

The Second Circuit has stated that "[t]he crucial time for accrual purposes is when the plaintiff becomes aware that he is suffering from a wrong for which damages may be recovered in a civil action."[425]

In *Eagleston v. Guido*,[426] the Second Circuit emphasized that where wrongful conduct involves multiple potential defendants, the district court should consider specifically as to each defendant at what point plaintiff had a compensable claim against each defendant.[427]

---

[422] *See id.*; *see also, Cada*, 920 F.2d at 451.

[423] *See Fitzgerald v. Barnstable Sch. Comm.*, 555 U.S. 246, 257 (2009) ("Title IX reaches institutions and programs that receive federal funds … but it has consistently been interpreted as not authorizing suit against school officials, teachers, and other individuals.").

[424] *See Cada*, 920 F.2d at 451.

[425] *Pinaud v. County of Suffolk*, 52 F.3d 1139, 1157 (2d Cir. 1995) (*citing, Singleton v. City of New York*, 632 F.2d 185,192-93 (2d Cir. 1980), *cert. denied*, 450 U.S. 920 (1981)).

[426] 41 F.3d 865 (2d Cir. 1994).

[427] *Id.* at 872.

The Second Circuit has also stated that it has not created a "Catch-22" accrual standard for federal actions.[428] "[We] do[ ] not require[ ] a plaintiff to bring a claim of which he ... neither knows nor ought to know ... [S]imply [put,] ... when a plaintiff knows or ought to know of a wrong, the statute of limitations on that claim starts to run[.]"[429]

The federal discovery rule may thus delay the accrual of a Title IX claim of sexual harassment (based on sexual assault)—under appropriate circumstances—even where the plaintiff failed to conduct any investigation against his school after he knew that (and when) he had been sexually abused, the identity of the abuser, and that the abuser was employed by the school.

F.   Since the Injury in a Title IX Sex Abuse Claim is a Violation of a Student's Civil Rights, Such Claims Accrue When a Plaintiff Knows or Should Know That His Civil Rights Have Been Violated

Several federal courts have used the federal discovery rule to determine when federal claims based upon sexual abuse should accrue.[430] Each of these cases deserves careful scrutiny.

In *Lamy*, a former public school student brought an action against a city, public school officials, a teacher, and the teacher's family, alleging federal and state civil rights violations and common-law torts based on the teacher's alleged sexual

---

[428] *Pinaud*, 52 F.3d at 1156.

[429] *Id.*

[430] *Armstrong v. Lamy ("Lamy")*, 938 F. Supp. 1018 (D. Ma. 1996); *Doe v. Bd. of Educ. of Hononegah Comm. High School Dist.*, 833 F. Supp. 1366 (N.D. Ill. 1993); *Sowers v. Bradford Area School Dist.*, 694 F. Supp. 125 (W.D. Pa. 1988), *vacated on other grounds, Smith v. Sowers*, 490 U.S. 1002 (1989).

abuse of the student.[431] The plaintiff pled claims under 42 U.S.C. § 1983 against the principal, the superintendent of schools, members of the school committee, and the City of Peabody (collectively, the "Municipal Defendants").[432] He did not bring a § 1983 claim against the teacher.[433]

The *Lamy* Court borrowed Massachusetts' three year statute of limitations for personal injury actions [Mass. Gen. L. ch. 260, § 2A], and noted that federal law applicable to § 1983 claims also borrows the state's principles for tolling the limitations period.[434]

The dispute in *Lamy* focused on when the three year statute of limitations began to run, which governed when plaintiff's Section 1983 claims accrued.[435] *Lamy* correctly observed that although the limitation period is determined as a matter of state law, the accrual date of a Section 1983 action is determined as a matter of federal law.[436]

Under the federal "discovery rule," Section 1983 claims accrue when the plaintiff "knows or has reason to know of the injury which is the basis of the cause of action."[437]

---

[431] 938 F. Supp. at 1025.

[432] *Id.* at 1031.

[433] *Id.*

[434] *Id.* at 1032 (*citing, Bd. of Regents v. Tomanio*, 446 U.S. 478, 483-86 (1980)).

[435] *Id.*

[436] *Id.* (*citing, inter alia, LaFont-Rivera v. Soler-Zapata*, 984 F.2d 1, 2-3 (1st Cir. 1993)).

[437] *Id.* (*citing, inter alia, Calero-Colon v. Betancourt-Lebron*, 68 F.3d 1, 3 (1st Cir. 1995); *Lavellee v. Listi*, 611 F.2d 1129, 1131 (5th Cir. 1980) (in § 1983 actions, "until the plaintiff is in possession of the 'critical facts that he has been hurt and who has inflicted the injury,' … the statute of limitations does not commence to run.") (*citing, U.S. v. Kubrick*, 444 U.S. 111, 122 (1979) (discovery rule under Federal Tort Claims Act)).

Lamy stated that if plaintiff's Section 1983 claim were against the alleged abuser teacher based on the abuser's injury to plaintiff's constitutional rights, the question as to when he knew or had reason to know of his injury under the federal discovery rule would be different from the question then before the Court.[438]

> The theory of [plaintiff's] claim against the Municipal Defendants is not that [plaintiff] was sexually abused by any person among the Municipal Defendants, but that the Municipal Defendants created the circumstances under which another person, a teacher, sexually abused him. In other words, [plaintiff's] § 1983 claim against the Municipal Defendants is that, if the Municipal Defendants had taken action to prevent teachers from abusing students, [the abuser teacher] would not have abused [plaintiff].[439]

The *Lamy* Court cited several district courts in other jurisdictions which held that the date the claim accrued against school officials was different from the date the claim accrued against the alleged abuser, because "a plaintiff could not reasonably be expected to know that the conduct of the school officials was a cause of the injury and violation of his constitutional rights."[440] *Lamy* thus adopted plaintiff's argument that summary judgment against the Municipal Defendants was "not appropriate on the issue of the statute of limitation" because the evidence did not indicate the date on which plaintiff knew or should have known that the Municipal Defendants—by allegedly

---

[438] *Id.*

[439] *Id.*

[440] *Id.* at 1033 (citations omitted).

failing to supervise and control the abuser teacher and promulgating policies that permitted sexual abuse to flourish within the school system—were a proximate cause of plaintiff's injury, even though he knew that he had been abused by the teacher at issue.[441]

Similarly, in *Doe v. Board of Educ. of Hononegah Comm. High School Dist. #207*, (*"Hononegah"*), before the Northern District of Illinois Court, a student who was allegedly sexually abused by a teacher filed Section 1983 claims against members of school administrators, and school counselors.[442] The *Hononegah* Court applied the federal discovery rule and federal law and analyzed when plaintiff's federal claims accrued in response to defendants' motion to dismiss these claims on timeliness grounds.[443]

The Court framed the issue as whether, as a matter of law, "plaintiff knew or should have known that her constitutional rights were violated at the time of the last incident of sexual abuse against her while she was a minor student."[444] As plaintiff knew that she was abused, and knew her abuser, if plaintiff had pled a claim against the abuser based entirely on injuries arising from the sexual abuse, her claims, of course, would be time-barred.[445]

---

[441] *Id.* at 1033. When the *Lamy* Court examined the merits of plaintiff's Section 1983 claims against school officials, it dismissed them on the grounds that plaintiff failed to proffer sufficient evidence that any of the Municipal Defendants had knowledge that the teacher was sexually abusing a student, or demonstrated "deliberate indifference" to the teacher's offensive acts. *Id.* at 1033-35. *Lamy* likewise dismissed plaintiff's Section 1983 claim against the City of Peabody on the basis that plaintiff failed to proffer sufficient evidence that the city had implemented any municipal policy or custom which countenanced the sexual abuse of children. *Id.* at 1035-36.

[442] 833 F. Supp. at 1370-72.

[443] *Id.* at 1375.

[444] *Id.* at 1375.

[445] *Id.* at 1376.

Yet, the Court emphasized that the theory of her federal claims was "not simply that she was sexually abused but that she was abused by a teacher under circumstances created by defendant."[446] While she knew she was abused, there was nothing in her complaint to "remotely suggest that she knew or should have known of the alleged acts or omissions of defendants."[447] To the contrary, the complaint alleged "that defendants took action to conceal or cover-up the teacher's sexual misconduct."[448]

The *Hononegah* Court held that under those alleged circumstances, "it [was] not at all reasonable to expect a minor student to have effectively discovered such efforts by defendants."[449] As plaintiff had no reason to know that her constitutional rights had been violated, her federal claims did not accrue during the time period of her sexual abuse.[450] Her claims, therefore, were not barred by the statute of limitations.[451]

In *Sowers v. Bradford Area School Dist.*, likewise, the Western District of Pennsylvania Court held, in a Section 1983 case, that the federal discovery rule delayed the accrual of the applicable borrowed state statute of limitations, where a plaintiff who had been sexually assaulted by a teacher pled that a school district, superintendent, principal, and assistant principal had fostered a practice, custom, or policy of reckless indifference and/or active concealment of instances of known or suspected sexual abuse.[452]

Sowers observed accurately a key point that district courts often confuse or overlook: a court must consider the accrual of a cause of action as the threshold statute of limitations issue

---

[446] *Id.*
[447] *Id.*
[448] *Id.*
[449] *Id.*
[450] *Id.*
[451] *Id.*
[452] 694 F. Supp. at 132 & 138-39.

because any state tolling doctrine does "not come into play until the [federal] cause of action accrued."[453]

In *Sowers* the Court emphasized that plaintiff, who knew she had been sexually assaulted, alleged that she did not know the defendant school officials were the "cause of her injury" at the time she was assaulted.[454] There were no allegations in the complaint that plaintiff "knew of the defendants' handling of previous sex abuse complaints against teachers."[455] And, as the discovery rule delays accrual of a cause of action until a plaintiff knew or should have known the injury and its causal connection to the defendants, the applicable borrowed state statute of limitations[456] did not begin to run until the abuser teacher's history of sexual abuse (allegedly known but concealed by defendants) was revealed to the community in which plaintiff lived.[457]

The *Sowers* Court thus concluded that plaintiff was entitled to offer evidence to support her claim that she did not know, and should not have been expected to know, that there existed an environment of reckless indifference toward sexual abuse of female students by teachers in the subject school district.[458]

---

[453] *Id.* at 136.

[454] *Id.* at 138.

[455] *Id.*

[456] 42 Pa. C.S.A § 5524(2), which requires a plaintiff to assert a personal injury action within two (2) years of accrual.

[457] *Id. See also, Doe v. Paukstat*, 863 F. Supp. 884 (E.D. Wis. 1994) (in § 1983 school sexual abuse case against teacher and school district, summary judgment against the school district on the statute of limitation issue was denied where issues of disputed fact existed as to when student knew that she was injured by the school district's conduct of promulgating policies that fostered child abuse).

[458] *Id.* at 139. The United States Supreme Court vacated *Sowers, see Smith v. Sowers*, 490 U.S. 1002 (1989), and remanded to the Third Circuit for

Lamy, Hononegah, and *Sowers*, each involved public schools and thus triggered Section 1983 claims based upon alleged violations of the Equal Protection Clause of the Fourteenth Amendment. A question thus arises as to whether a Title IX sex abuse injury is a violation of a constitutional right.

The Second Circuit, in *Bruneau ex rel. Schofield v. South Kortright Cent. School Dist.*,[459] held that Title IX provides the exclusive remedial avenue to vindicate a student's "constitutional right to an educational environment free of sexual harassment[.]"[460] Accordingly, as plaintiff's claim that the school defendants violated her Equal Protection rights by failing to remedy ongoing discrimination on the basis of sex was "based on the same factual predicate as her Title IX claim," the Second Circuit ruled that plaintiff could "not maintain her § 1983 claim and thereby bypass the comprehensive remedial scheme created in Title IX." [*Id.*].

In *Fitzgerald v. Barnstable School Committee*,[461] the Supreme Court abrogated *Bruneau* and held that Title IX is not "the sole means of vindicating the constitutional right to be free from gender discrimination perpetrated by educational institutions."[462] As Title IX's protections are narrower than Section 1983's in some respects and broader in others, the Supreme Court

---

further consideration in light of *De Shaney v. Winnebago County Dept. of Social Services*, 489 U.S. 189 (1989). *De Shaney* does not address the statute of limitations issue, and the Third Circuit, upon remand, affirmed *Sowers* without a published opinion. *See Sowers v. Bradford Area School Dist.*, 887 F.2d 262 (3d Cir. 1989). As stated by the *Hononegah* Court, "[u]nder these circumstances, the district court's ruling on the statute of limitations issue [in *Sowers*] retains vitality." *Hononegah*, 833 F. Supp. at 1376 n. 9).

[459] 163 F.3d 749 (2d Cir. 1998).
[460] *Id.* at 758.
[461] 555 U.S. 246 (2009).
[462] *Id.* (citation omitted).

determined that Title IX should be interpreted to allow for parallel and concurrent Section 1983 claims.[463]

In *Gebser v. Lago Vista Indep. School Dist.*,[464] the Supreme Court emphasized that its "creation of a high standard for liability removes the risk that an employer would be responsible for its employees' independent actions, rather than its own 'official decision.'"[465] Moreover, "[c]omparable considerations led to our adoption of a deliberate indifference standard for claims under § 1983 alleging that a municipality's actions in failing to prevent a deprivation of federal rights was the cause of the violation."[466]

In view of *Gebser*, it is irrelevant for accrual purposes whether Title IX protects "constitutional" rights. At minimum, the injury in a Title IX sex abuse case is a violation of a unique civil right with constitutional implications—to be free of sexual harassment (through sexual abuse) perpetrated by an educational institution—which Congress created. Accordingly, pursuant to the reasoning of *Lamy, Hononegah, Sowers*, and scores of other cases which discuss constitutional injuries,[467] since the injury in a Title IX sexual abuse claim is the violation of a civil (if not constitutional) right, such claims accrue when a plaintiff knows or should know that his civil (and/or constitutional) rights have been violated.

---

[463] *Id.* at 258-59.
[464] 524 U.S. 274 (1998).
[465] *Id.* at 291.
[466] *Id.* at 290.
[467] *See e.g., Hawkinson v. Montoya*, 385 Fed. Appx. 836, 841 (10th Cir. 2010).

G. Federal Accrual Issues Are Easily Confused With New York Accrual Rules

As the Second Circuit emphasized in *Pearl*, New York federal and state courts have had great difficulty in reconciling accrual, which is governed by federal law, with tolling, which is governed by state law, when a plaintiff asserts fraudulent concealment of some kind.[468] The central problem "is that the reported decisions of the federal and state courts do not always mean the same things by their use of these phrases, and phrases to which some judges ascribe different meanings are used interchangeably by other judges."[469] The *Pearl* Court correctly identified, but underestimated, the extent of the problem.

The overlap between accrual and tolling based on fraudulent concealment creates confusion of a magnitude rarely seen in the federal courts. These issues, too often, seem as clear-cut as a riddle, shrouded in a puzzle, wrapped in an enigma.

A threshold problem is that under New York law "equitable tolling," is swallowed under the definition of "equitable estoppel."[470] The interchangeable terms equitable estoppel and equitable tolling, under New York law, permit a plaintiff to defeat a statute of limitations defense "when plaintiff

---

[468] 296 F. 3d at 81.

[469] *Id.*

[470] New York uses the label "equitable estoppel" to cover both the circumstances where the defendant conceals from the plaintiff the fact that he has a cause of action [and] where the plaintiff is aware of his cause of action, but the defendant induces him to forego suit until after the period of limitations has expired." *Pearl*, 296 F.3d at 82 (*citing, inter alia, Joseph M. McLaughlin, Practice Commentaries, N.Y. CPLR* C 201: 6 at 63 (McKinney 1990). In the Second Circuit, the former scenario is described as "equitable tolling," while the latter is deemed "equitable estoppel." *See Pearl*, 296 F.3d at 81.

was induced by fraud, misrepresentations, or deception to refrain from filing a timely action."[471]

The term "equitable tolling" under New York law, may thus not be invoked to prevent a statute of limitations from beginning to run. The law of accrual governs that scenario and New York law, with limited exceptions, applies a general accrual rule, which holds that "mere ignorance or lack of discovery of the wrong is not sufficient to toll the statute of limitations, which commences running when the wrong is perpetuated."[472] The New York Court of Appeals has likewise stated that "a tort cause of action cannot accrue until an injury is sustained ... That, rather than the wrongful act of defendant or discovery of the injury by plaintiff, is the relevant date for marking accrual."[473]

Moreover, under New York law, as discussed above, "equitable estoppel does not apply where the misrepresentation or act of concealment underlying the estoppel claim is the same act which forms the basis of plaintiff's underlying cause of action."[474] Instead, for equitable estoppel to be triggered, a plaintiff must establish that a defendant made fraudulent misrepresentations or otherwise engaged in overt misconduct— *after his initial wrongdoing*—which prevented plaintiff from

---

[471] *See Abbas v. Dixon*, 480 F.3d 636, 642 (2d Cir. 2007) (citations omitted); *Statler, D.C. v. Dell, Inc.*, 841 F. Supp. 2d 642, 647 (EDNY 2012) (under New York law, the terms "equitable tolling" and "equitable estoppel" are interchangeable); *City of Syracuse v. Loomis Armored US, LLC*, 2012 WL 4491119 (NDNY 2012) (same).

[472] *General Stencils, Inc. v. Ciappa*, 18 N.Y.2d 125, 127 (1966).

[473] *Kronos, Inc. v. AVX Corp*, 81 N.Y.2d 90, 94 (1993).

[474] *See* Chapter I.B, *infra; Abercrombie v. Andrew College*, 438 F. Supp.2d 243, 265 (SDNY 2006) (*quoting, Kaufman v. Cohen*, 307 A.D.2d 113, 122 (1st Dept. 2003); *see also, Ross v. Louise Wise Services, Inc.*, 8 N.Y.3d 478, 491 (2d Dept. 2007).

commencing her action on time.[475]

This equitable estoppel doctrine, pursuant to New York common law, thus provides that if a plaintiff alleges fraudulent concealment which occurred *prior* to or concurrent with the cause of action sued upon, then he may not invoke equitable estoppel or equitable tolling to stop or toll the applicable statute of limitations.

If, however, a plaintiff's complaint sounds in fraud, then he can invoke the fraud discovery-diligence rule, CPLR § 213(8), which provides that a plaintiff must sue for fraud no later than two (2) years from the date he discovered, or with reasonable diligence could have discovered, the fraud. A plaintiff's fraud claim in New York thus accrues (i.e., the statute of limitations starts to run) only when he discovers or should (through reasonable diligence) have discovered the fraud.[476]

New York's statutory accrual rule for fraud actions [CPLR § 213(8)] mirrors Judge Posner's admonition in *Cada*:

> Equitable estoppel in the limitations setting is sometimes called fraudulent concealment, but must not be confused with efforts by a defendant in a fraud case to conceal the fraud. To the extent that such efforts succeed, they postpone the date of accrual by preventing the plaintiff from discovering that he is a victim of a fraud...They are thus within the domain of the [federal] discovery rule.[477]

The Second Circuit uses a more expansive definition of equitable tolling, holding that it means both fraudulent

---

[475] *Abercrombie*, 438 F. Supp.2d at 265; *Kaufman*, 307 A.D.2d at 122; *Ross*, 8 N.Y.3d at 491; *Zumpano v. Quinn*, 6 N.Y.3d at 674-75; *Rizk v. Cohen*, 73 N.Y.2d at 105-06 (1989); *Smith v. Smith*, 830 F.2d at 13.
[476] *See* Chapters I.F and II.F, *supra*.
[477] 920 F.2d at 451.

concealment of a cause of action that has "in some sense accrued earlier,"[478] and fraudulent concealment that postpones the accrual of a cause of action.[479] The Second Circuit's loose use of accrual language under an "equitable tolling" label threatens to blur—for litigants, attorneys, and judges—the distinctions between the two terms beyond all recognition.

The evolved or, more accurately, devolved, Second Circuit "equitable tolling" doctrine covers fraudulent concealment that occurs both *before* and *after* the initial wrongdoing, and demonstrates that the Second Circuit's uneven application of the doctrine is quite different from—and easily confused with—New York common law (which strictly and consistently limits "equitable tolling" to conduct which occurs *after* the initial wrongdoing).[480]

The substantial confusion over the proper use of the terms "equitable estoppel" or "equitable tolling" should nevertheless not obscure Judge Posner's simple but critical accrual lesson: Federal courts, when engaging in a threshold determination as to when a federal claim accrued, in the face of fraudulent concealment allegations, need to ascertain only whether the alleged fraud—whether committed before or after the initial fraud—was made to conceal the defendant's initial wrongful act. If defendant's fraudulent concealment prevents a

---

[478] *See Pinaud v. County of Suffolk*, 52 F.3d 1139, 1156 (2d Cir. 1995).

[479] *See Cerbone v. Int'l Ladies' Garment Workers' Union*, 76 F.2d 45, 48 (2d Cir. 1985) ("Under this doctrine [of equitable tolling], the statute does not begin to run until the plaintiff either acquires actual knowledge of the facts that comprise his cause of action or should have acquired such knowledge through the exercise of reasonable diligence."); *see also*, *Pearl*, 296 F.3d at 82; *Keating*, 706 F.2d at 382 (also using accrual language— "the time does not begin running"—while invoking the "equitable tolling" doctrine).

[480] *See* notes 27-30, *supra*, and accompanying text.

plaintiff from discovering *that defendant injured her*, the federal discovery rule, which concerns accrual issues, not equitable tolling or equitable estoppel, should be triggered.[481]

H.   A Plaintiff May Establish that His Title IX Claim Did Not Accrue If He Can Colorably Claim that School Officials Concealed from Him Critical Facts Related to the School's Own Culpable Conduct Which Led to His Sex Abuse by a School Employee

The federal courts have long applied the discovery rule for accrual when a tortfeasor has interfered with a victim's rights through fraud or concealment.[482] A plaintiff is thus deemed to have notice of his claim such that his cause of action accrues when he "has or with reasonable diligence should have discovered the critical facts of both his injury and its cause."[483]

The element of causation is critical to a proper analysis of when a plaintiff's Title IX claim based on a school's cover-up of sex abuse accrued. Numerous courts have held that even though a plaintiff's injury may be well known and understood by the plaintiff, his tort claim does not accrue until he at least has sufficient information to determine the party responsible for that

---

[481] *See Cada*, 920 F.2d at 451; *see also, Martin v. Consultants & Admins., Inc.*, 966 F.2d 1078, 1104 n.17 (7th Cir. 1992) (*citing, Cada*, 920 F.2d at 450-51)("Self-concealing frauds ... do not extend the statute of limitations pursuant to a tolling doctrine, but 'postpone the date of accrual by preventing the plaintiff from discovering that he is a victim of fraud,'... thus implicating the 'discovery rule' of federal common law.")).

[482] *See Peck v. U.S.*, 470 F. Supp. 1003, 1018 (SDNY 1979); *Fitzgerald v. Seamans*, 553 F.2d 220, 228 (D.C. Cir. 1977).

[483] *Kronisch v. U.S.*, 150 F.3d 112, 121 (2d Cir. 1998). *See also, Rotella v. Wood*, 528 U.S. 549, 555 (2000)(Under the discovery rule, a claim accrues when a plaintiff comes into possession of the "critical facts that he has been hurt *and who inflicted the injury*.")(emphasis added).

injury.[484]

Barrett v. U.S. is particularly enlightening. There, plaintiff, the estate of a man who died in 1953, sued the United States under 42 U.S.C. § 1983 and the Federal Tort Claims Act ("FTCA") on the bases that the Government was negligent in implementing an Army chemical warfare experiment *and* engaged in a conspiracy to cover up the cause of plaintiff's decedent's death.[485] The estate filed suit shortly after the Secretary of the Army revealed, in 1975, that decedent, a male civilian voluntarily undergoing treatment at a New York hospital, died from the injection of a mescaline derivative given to him while he unknowingly served as a test subject in an Army chemical warfare experiment.[486]

The Second Circuit held that a genuine material issue of fact existed as to the extent of the Government's concealment of material facts relating to the Army's responsibility for decedent's death and denied the Government's summary judgment motion in which it argued that, as a matter of law, plaintiff's FTCA cause of action was time-barred under the applicable two year statute of limitations.[487]

The Second Circuit noted that since the injury was immediately known, the implicated issue was "when the decedent's family should have discovered the critical facts relating to the cause of his death."[488] The *Barrett* Court also stated that

---

[484] *See e.g.*, *Valdez v. U.S.*, 518 F.3d 173, 178 (2d Cir. 2008) (in determining accrual date of medical malpractice claim brought under Federal Tort Claims Act, 28 U.S.C. § 2401 (b), notice to plaintiff must be of doctor-caused harm, but does not have to be of negligent doctor-caused harm); *see also, Barrett v. U.S.*, 689 F.2d 324, 327-28 (2d Cir. 1982).

[485] *Id.* at 328.

[486] *Id.*

[487] *Id.* at 328-29.

[488] *Id.* at 328 (emphasis added).

the "critical facts about causation ... were in the control of the Government and very difficult for his estate to obtain."[489] As various critical facts pertaining to causation "would not have been revealed no matter how diligently the estate had pursued its case in the 1950s," the Court concluded that the accrual issue (or when the applicable statute began to run) was a factual issue which needed to be resolved at trial.[490]

The *Barrett* Court emphasized that the facts before it were similar to those presented in *Ware v. U.S.*[491] In that case,

> The Department of Agriculture had mistakenly found Ware's cattle to be suffering from tuberculosis and ordered them killed. Ware was permitted to sue the Government more than two years (the applicable statute of limitations period) after the event. He immediately knew of the injury, the death of his cattle, and its direct cause, that they were put to death. The critical fact that he did not know until later was that they need not have been slaughtered.[492]

An examination of the facts in a hypothetical school sex abuse cover-up case begets both a similar analysis and conclusion. Plaintiffs immediately knew of the injury, their sexual abuse, and its direct cause, their sex abuser. But the critical fact that they did not know until later was that they would not have been sexually abused if their school and its officials had fulfilled their most basic and important duty: to protect the children in their care.[493]

---

[489] *Id.* at 329.

[490] *Id.*

[491] 626 F.2d 1278 (5th Cir. 1980)

[492] *Id.* at 329-330; *see Ware*, 626 F.2d at 1284-85.

[493] *See also, Hononegah*, 833 F. Supp. at 1376 (plaintiff knew that she was abused but did not know or should have known of the alleged acts or

Plaintiffs who can plausibly allege a colorable school conspiracy by school officials to conceal a school's culpability with respect to the sexual abuse of children in its charge should thus be able to successfully plead that the accrual of their Title IX claims should be delayed until the school's role in their sexual abuse (i.e., the necessary causation element of their Title IX claims) is publicly revealed.[494]

The federal discovery rule, when applied to a Title IX claim in a school sex abuse cover-up case, should thus delay accrual of a plaintiff's Title IX claim (i.e., the running of the borrowed three year state statute of limitation for personal injury actions [CPLR § 214(5)] until the time that plaintiff discovered, or could have discovered, that: (1) an official of the school who had authority to institute corrective measures on the school's behalf had actual notice of a teacher's proclivities for sexual abuse; and (2) the school, in the face of that actual notice, was deliberately indifferent to the teacher's misconduct.[495]

The issue is not whether or when a plaintiff knew she had been sexually abused *by the teacher*. Rather, it is when did the plaintiff know or should have known that her civil rights were violated *by the school*.[496] In other words, the statute of limitations

---

omissions of school officials); *Sowers*, 694 F. Supp. at 138 (plaintiff knew she had been sexually assaulted, but—because she did not know that the school had previously handled sexual abuse complaints against her abuser teacher—she did not know that the school officials were the "cause of her injury.")

[494] *See Yeadon v. NYC Transit Auth.*, 719 F. Supp. 204, 209 (SDNY 1989)("A plaintiff with knowledge of one claim but deprived of information critical to another claim may still invoke these tolls [including delayed accrual when defendants' fraudulent conduct may have deprived plaintiff of information essential to the formulation of his claims] to save the claims about which he could not have known.").

[495] *See Tesoriero*, 382 F. Supp.2d at 396; *Zamora*, 414 F. Supp.2d at 424.

[496] *See Hononegah*, 833 F. Supp. at 1375.

on plaintiff's Title IX claim should not start to run until plaintiff knew or should have known that the school created the circumstances in which another person, the offending teacher, abused her.[497]

The federal discovery accrual rule for plaintiffs' Title IX claims closely resembles the New York accrual rule [CPLR § 213(8)] for fraud actions. Both provide that a plaintiff may plausibly allege that a school's concealment of its own misconduct, even without any post-abuse fraud, misrepresentations, or deception, may have prevented him from discovering the school's role in his sexual abuse (i.e., the school's pre-abuse fraud).

Unlike in a fraud action, however, a plaintiff seeking redress in a Title IX sex abuse claim need not plead and prove "scienter" (intent to defraud). A school's concealment of its deliberate indifference in the face of actual knowledge of its employee's propensity to abuse children should suffice to delay accrual of a victim's Title IX claims against his culpable school.

---

[497] *See Lamy*, 938 F. Supp. at 1032-33.

I.   A Fact Is Not Deemed "Discovered" Until a Plaintiff Has Sufficient Information About That Fact to Plead It in a Complaint

In *SEC v. Wyly*,[498] District Judge Shira A. Scheindlin clarified the scope of the federal discovery rule in the wake of *Merck*. There, the Court reaffirmed that the discovery rule applies "where a plaintiff has been injured by fraud and remains in ignorance of it without any fault or want of diligence or care on his part."[499]

> In such cases, 'the bar of the statute does not begin to run until the fraud is discovered, *though there be no special circumstances or efforts on the part of the party committing the fraud to conceal it from the knowledge of the other party.*' [500]

"The date of discovery for purposes of the discovery rule, is the earliest of 'when the litigant first knows or with due diligence should know the facts that will form the basis for an action.'"[501]

Judge Scheindlin noted that the Second Circuit recently clarified that under *Merck*, "a fact is not deemed 'discovered' until a reasonably diligent plaintiff would have sufficient information about that fact to adequately plead it in a complaint. In other words, the reasonably diligent plaintiff has not 'discovered' one of the facts constituting a [statutory] violation until he can plead that fact with sufficient detail and particularity to survive a 12(b)(6) motion to dismiss."[502]

---

[498] 788 F. Supp.2d 92 (SDNY 2011).

[499] *Id.* at 103.

[500] *Id.* (*quoting, Holmberg*, 327 U.S. at 396-97) (emphasis added).

[501] *Id.* (*citing, Merck*, 130 S. Ct. at 1793).

[502] *Id.* (*quoting, City of Pontiac Gen. Employees' Retirement Sys. v. MBIA, Inc.*, 637 F.3d 169, 174-75 (2d Cir. 2011)).

A plaintiff's Title IX claim will not accrue, therefore, until he discovers or could through reasonable diligence have discovered the basic elements of his Title IX claim to the extent necessary to plead them in a complaint.[503]

When a school conceals its initial wrongdoing, by simply keeping a known sex predator as a teacher or coach on staff, or by failing to report allegations of that employee's sexual abuse of a child to law enforcement authorities, it will be extremely difficult for defendants to establish (particularly at the pleading stage) that a plaintiff knew or should have known of the school's own misconduct which gives rise to Title IX liability.

If every action taken by a school where a student is sexually assaulted indicates that the school's administrators believe the abusive teacher is a trustworthy member of the faculty in good-standing with the school community, the law does not mandate that an abused student, by osmosis or otherwise, must somehow ferret out the concealed (and/or misrepresented) truth.[504]

---

[503] *See id*; *see also*, CPLR § 3013, which mandates that "[s]tatements in a pleading shall be sufficiently particular to give the court and parties notice of the transactions, occurrences, or series of transactions or occurrences, intended to be proven and the material elements of each cause of action[.]"; *Peri v. State of New York*, 66 A.D.2d 949, 949 (3d Dept. 1978) ("[a]t a minimum, a valid complaint must include all material elements of the cause of action."); *East Hampton Union Free School Dist. v. Sandpebble Builders, Inc.*, 66 A.D.3d 122, 127 (2d Dept. 2009) (same); *Residents for a More Beautiful Port Washington, Inc. v. Town of Hempstead*, 153 A.D.3d 727, 729 (2d Dept. 1989) (for a plaintiff to survive a motion to dismiss for failure to state a cause of action, the factual allegations in the complaint cannot be "merely conclusory and speculative in nature and not supported by any specific facts.").

[504] This is particularly true in light of the well-documented, severe, and often long-lasting, emotional and psychological problems that sexually abused children face after they are abused.

The proper application of the federal discovery rule in a school sex abuse cover-up case brought under Title IX will thus prevent a school from benefiting from any conspiracy or cover-up designed to conceal from former students, students, parents, and prospective students, the fact that the school continued to employ a teacher or coach, even after the school *knew* that such an employee was a sexual predator. Such a result is well-grounded in both law and equity.

CONCLUSION

As the New York Court of Appeals noted in the context of a statute of limitations analysis, "[c]ourts and legislatures need not be viewed as antagonists in the area of tort law."[505] To the contrary "[d]eveloping the law is the province of both, and the peculiar attributes of these institutions are complementary in getting the task performed. Judicial action is often necessary to bring to the attention of the Legislature a particular problem in order for it to accomplish the necessary reform which only legislative action can fashion."[506]

New York federal and state judges thus do not need to wait for legislative action to provide an equitable legal remedy for individuals sexually abused by school employees after school officials *knowingly* turned a blind eye and deaf ear to horrors inflicted upon children in their care. For intellectual succor, they can start by examining the words of a Roman philosopher who has been dead for more than two thousand years.

---

[505] *Flanagan v. Mount Eden General Hosp.*, 24 N.Y.2d 427, 435 (1969) (citations omitted).
[506] *Id.*

Until his assassination in 44 B.C., Marcus Tullius Cicero, a renowned Roman lawyer and political thinker, strove to discover a proper framework for good laws, sound government, and the political and legal formula for human beings to peacefully and happily co-exist.[507] His writings on Natural Law profoundly influenced the Founding Fathers as they pushed, pulled and strained to form a new government, built upon a foundation of just laws, for the people.[508]

Cicero defined Natural Law as "true law," which is "right agreement with nature."[509] "[Natural Law, therefore] is the distinction between things just and unjust, made in agreement with that primal and most ancient of things, Nature; and in conformity to Nature's standard are framed those human laws which inflict punishment upon the wicked and protect the good."[510]

Marci A. Hamilton, a law professor at the Benjamin N. Cardozo School of Law, Yeshiva University, seeks to add a modern page to Cicero's ancient playbook. *In Justice Denied: What America Must Do to Protect Its Children*,[511] Professor Hamilton proposes a comprehensive solution to ameliorate the scourge of childhood sexual abuse: eliminate the arbitrary statutes of limitations so that survivors past and present can get fair redress from courts.

---

[507] W. Cleon Skousen, *The Five Thousand Year Leap* (American Documents Publishing, LLC 1981, 2009 at 33).

[508] *See id.* at 33-40.

[509] *See id.* at 35.

[510] *Id.* at 39 (citation omitted).

[511] (Cambridge University Press 2008).

Professor Hamilton states that "arbitrary and unjust" statutes of limitation have "made it easy for perpetrators to move from child to child, and state to state, with confidence that they will not be punished for the horrors inflicted on the last child."[512]

"The reality is that it often takes *decades* for a child sex abuse survivor to come forward to family, friends, a spouse, or the authorities."[513] As such, "the legal system usually works for the predator and against the survivor (and the rest of us) because of the arbitrary [statutes of limitation] that keep the courthouse doors locked."[514]

Cicero presciently described how legislation, if contrary to Natural Law, can foster grave injustice:

> [T]he most foolish notion of all is the belief that everything is just which is found in the customs or laws of nations ... What of the many deadly, the many pestilential statutes which nations put in force? These no more deserve to be called laws than the rules a band of robbers might pass in their assembly. For if ignorant and unskilled men have prescribed deadly poisons instead of healing drugs, these cannot possibly be called physicians' prescriptions; neither in a nation can a statute of any sort be called a law, even though the nation, in spite of being a ruinous regulation has accepted it.[515]

---

[512] *Id.* at 13.

[513] *Id.* at 18 (citations omitted) (emphasis in original).

[514] *Id.* at 20.

[515] Skousen at 38 (*citing*, William Ebenstein, *Great Political Thinkers* (Rinehart 1951), at 134).

Professor Hamilton notes that the introduction of more women (and, therefore, mothers) in the legislatures has finally pushed children's issues towards the top of various states' legislative agendas.[516] One such mother-legislator is the intrepid Queens Assemblywoman Margaret M. Markey, who has sponsored proposed legislation, The Child Victims Act, in the New York State Assembly every year since 2006.

The latest iteration of The Child Victims Act (A. 1771/S. 03809) would end the statute of limitations for all sexual abuse crimes against children and also allow a one-year window for adults who were sexually abused as children to file lawsuits against their abusers and their abusers' enablers.[517] This bill (which remains locked in legislative limbo), if passed, would radically alter the landscape in New York for "old" sexual abuse cases against culpable schools and school officials.

Unless and until that right-minded bill or a comparable version becomes law, however, judges presented with school sex abuse cover-up cases should not merely throw up their hands, bemoan the absurdity and unfairness of the extant legal scheme, defer to the New York State Legislature, and throw grievously injured plaintiffs out of court. These judges, while the proverbial Rome burns, need not fiddle.

---

[516] *See* Hamilton at 20.

[517] *See* Jessica String, *Rally planned to push for Child Victims Act*, April 15, 2013,   Legislativegazette.com,   available   at: *http://www.legislativegazette.com/Articles-Top-Stories-c-2013-04-15-83.*

New York state and federal judges, rather, should keep close to heart Cicero's creed that true law, Natural Law, just law, must protect the good and punish the wicked.[518] As this book demonstrates, in "old" sex abuse cases involving school cover-ups for sexual predators, courts have a variety of jurisprudential weapons, culled from long-standing and widely recognized legal principles, to dispense real justice. Armed with such a solid and diverse legal foundation for both "righteous" and "right" decisions, courts should take pains to not protect the wicked and punish the good.

The time has come for sexual abuse litigation in New York State to emerge from the dark ages. For starters, schools and school officials must know, with close to metaphysical certainty, that if they cover up for sexually abusive employees and thus allow more innocent children to be sexually assaulted, they—the schools and culpable school officials—will suffer an appropriate (and steep) penalty.

The time has come for justice. Within this legislative scheme or the next.

Sexual abuse survivors have waited long enough.

---

[518] *See* Skousen at 39.

INDEX OF AUTHORITIES CITED

STATUTES & REGULATIONS:

BOOKS, TREATISES, & ARTICLES:

ABOUT THE AUTHOR

Kevin Thomas Mulhearn has practiced law in the state and federal courts in New York State since 1990. He was the lead attorney for the twelve plaintiffs in *Zimmerman v. Poly Prep Country Day School,* a landmark case filed in the U.S. District Court for the Eastern District of New York in which the Court denied the school defendants' motion to dismiss the case on timeliness grounds. (Plaintiffs alleged that they were abused by the school's football coach for various periods from the 1960s through the 1980s, but did not file suit until October 2009). Mr Mulhearn has represented, and continues to represent, dozens of adults who allege that they were sexually and/or physically abused as children at other private schools in New York such as The Horace Mann School, The Marsha Stern Talmudical Academy–Yeshiva University High School for Boys, St. Francis Preparatory School, and The New York School for the Deaf (Fanwood). Mr. Mulhearn has also written several guest columns for *The New York Daily News* on the Penn State sex abuse scandal. He lives in a suburb north of New York City.

QUICK ORDER FORM

Email Orders: orders@hardnockpress.com

Fax Orders: 1-845-398-3836. Send this form.

Telephone orders: 845-398-2734

Postal Orders: Hard Nock Press, LLC
                              P.O. Box 665
                              Orangeburg, NY 10962 (USA)

See our website (www.hardnockpress.com) for free information on other Books, Speaking/Seminars, Mailing Lists, Consulting.

ORDERING INFORMATION

Name:

Address:

City, State, Postal code:

Telephone No.:

Email:

Payment-   Check: Credit Card:
                                 Visa   MasterCard   AMEX

Card Number:
Name on card:
Expiration Date (mm/yy):
Security Code:

www.ingramcontent.com/pod-product-compliance
Lightning Source LLC
Chambersburg PA
CBHW061308220326
41599CB00026B/4782